the
ruby slipper
principles

the ruby
slipper principles

overcome self-doubt
release your inner power
create a life fulfilled

LOREEN MUZIK

Visit the author's website at: LoreenMuzik.com

ISBN: 9781731247537

1st edition, November 2018

the ruby slipper principles

A captivating action/adventure guide to self-illumination. Discover how to navigate your soul as you uncover your heroic journey, tap into the magic of your Universal GPS, and unleash the power of your ruby slippers.

"The biggest adventure you can ever take is to live the life of your dreams." ~ Oprah Winfrey

dedication

To you, a beautiful, energized spirit who is ready to breathe life into your infinite power, elevate your spiritual energy, and illuminate your being to light the way for yourself and others to prosper in magical ways – *to inspiralluminate.*

May this book provide you with the inspiration to honor your purpose and value, passion forward your gifts and elevate the vibrations of this planet by loving and shining your unique and beautiful light.

I wish for you the ultimate freedom – to be, do and have all that you desire in this life.

Loreen

acknowledgments

In deep gratitude to my original inspiration partner Nina East, for her gifted extraction of the genius I didn't know I had within me; my mirror MarciaAnn Lubore for whom I channeled this beautiful Oznalogy upon her insistence that I help her better understand her own heroic journey, and because 'you push me'; my dearest partner in divination Jay VanProyen who held space for me, consoled me, encouraged me and never let me give up on this dream; my intervention team Dawn Baeckeroot and Carolyn Kristoff without whom you'd NOT be reading this book right now; and finally to the love of my life, Jerry Muzik, you are my True Companion, I love you 1FST and I could NOT be who I am today without your unconditional love, support and infinite inspiration. I am truly blessed.

foreword

Does it seem to you that the chaos in the outer world permeates your experience? Have you noticed that the more you focus on it the more it persists and even grows in its influence? If so, you may be wondering how you can shift your trajectory and live fulfilled in a world that seems otherwise on the brink of collapse.

If you are drawn to spiritual or personal exploration I believe you are here to help usher in higher consciousness and true peace on earth. Welcome! We need you because, these are indeed uncertain and tumultuous times.

Like many, you may be longing for clarity, direction, inspiration and advice to live a more fulfilled and joyful life. If so, you are in for a great adventure.

The Ruby Slipper Principles are here to help you navigate this world from within and co-create a new experience.

If you're feeling a bit woozy because the tornado just dropped you in a foreign land with an angry witch out to steal your shoes... a bit discombobulated because you now seem to be surrounded by munchkins in their hypnotic rhythm, singing you tales of lollipops and gumdrops... and you're completely uncertain how you got here and how you'll get home... then you've come to the right place.

Allow me to be your Good Witch, Glinda, as I guide you along the yellow brick road that is your adventure to self-illumination, passion and fulfillment.

what you'll find within

THE RUBY SLIPPER PRINCIPLES

BACK TO KANSAS

read this first!
not just another shelf-help book

Before we delve into Oz, let me share with you how to navigate the yellow brick road you are about to see unfold before you.

NOT Just another Shelf-Help Book!

If you're anything like me you've purchased an entire library of self-help, motivational, inspirational, personal development and prosperity heightening books!

I love books, I LOVE being inspired and more than anything I LOVE when a book gives me a new perspective, opens a portal for me, ignites that ah-ha moment, the clarity I needed in that moment to see the next brick of the yellow brick road unfold before me. THAT is when a book becomes more than a bunch of words on the page and becomes the Lion, with the courage to act, on an adventure to Oz!

How often do you take COURAGEOUS action as suggested in the books? Do you do ponder the questions asked; journal the insights; write down the strategies, take the actual steps along the yellow brick road as outlined for you?

Or do you plow through those books, jot down a couple of passages and then put that book up on the shelf, perhaps to be referenced again another day.

Please don't let this become your next Shelf-Help book! There is no clicking your heels if you're stuck in Munchkinland.

You have already picked up this book... now, what's the best way to ensure you don't put it down without gaining at least some insight; a wonderful gold nugget, an ah-ha moment or even a real release of something that's been holding you back? First, have FUN with it and then, take action immediately on ANYTHING that resonates with you as you are reading.

Now I'm not one to tell you that you must read from front to back or read the entire book before you've gained 'the secret'... NOPE. I want you to use this as a joyful reference and do that however MOST resonates with you. If you want to read the whole thing in one sitting, absorb it all and then go back and ponder the most recent ah-ha moment you had – GREAT. If you want to peruse the table of contents and just grab hold of a chapter that looks interesting to you – do that! If you want to use it like you would bibliomancy (divination using books) do so by simply asking *"Where am I in my journey to Oz and what do I need to know right now?"* - then pick up this book, flip through the pages (or scroll of course if you're reading this electronically – or tap on the table of contents or what have you) stopping wherever you feel moved and... see what message reveals itself for you today... ALL of these methods of engagement are VALID and can be quite effective for you.

From the start you should be able to get a feel for the language of Oz (if not jump to the *archetypes of oz* or the *Oznalogy* as good starting points) and begin seeing it from a new perspective. Jot down quotes or phrases that speak loudly to you in the moment, heck, grab your little sticky notes and create a parade of flags set to march you through the adventure.

Throughout your exploration... ask yourself, where you are in your journey to Oz? What Principle most resonates with you in this moment? Then go take courageous action on *that Principle.*

There are questions begging for your consideration throughout this book, write down the answers.

> ♔ ***Super cool manifestation tip***: want to know how to create something out of nothing? WRITE IT DOWN. It just went from the ethers to your thoughts and then BOOM it's a thing in 3D when you write it down. Just like this book, from ethers to thought to written word and now... book! Cool right?

There are two characters who always beg for you to interact with them, Glinda (your Higher Self) and Toto (your intuition and imagination). Please promise to nurture your relationships with them... I promise they will lead you to buckets of water to throw on your Wicked Witches!

If, however, you set this book on a shelf (leave it unattended in your Kindle) and hope that the magic of reading it will be enough to have you clicking your heels, you are about to find out how misguided you are. You will find yourself stuck in Munchkinland – instead of being nourished by the actions you take throughout the book – you'll be offered gumdrops and lollipops which in the long run are NOT soul nourishing and... I hear from my father, a retired Dentist, cause decay!

To master the Ruby Slipper Principles, you must engage with them. USE them or lose them to your shelf.

Don't let the gems within fade away; do not allow the flying monkeys to capture your friends or the Wicked Witch to take away your shoes. Stay awake in the poppies or at least jot down a quick note if you are reading the book and start to feel sleepy OR like you want to put it down and not go back to it for a while... there are profound insights there for you I promise. Within those moments, lies the snow to come wake you up and get you back on track to your dreams fulfilled.

The moral of your story awaits you, the infinite power of your ruby slippers ready to be revealed, and most importantly, OTHERS are awaiting you and your light. As I type this, they are searching for you, for the beautiful guidance you offer them when you come back to share your adventure. When you finally click your heels and find your way home, you can then become Glinda for the next journey. Think of all the Dorothys you can help!

Can you imagine if Dorothy simply held on to the cellar doors? What then of her life and the lives of those in Oz?

I will ask of you now, please avoid the cellar. Cellar seekers are not able to click their heels and find the gold at the end of their rainbow. You are meant for so much more.

Master these principles; change your life and then passion-it-forward.

In fact, let's get you well on your way with an early win... a taste of your phenomenal ruby slippers.

Try this...

Take 3 deep breaths in and out right now. Focus on your desire to reveal your ruby slippers. Call Glinda to the top of your head (trust me... just do it... it works).

Now ask Glinda, "What is the message you have for me today?"

Close your eyes, visualize Glinda in her bubble above your head and be patient.

Now scroll through this book, however you like, stopping when you feel you are ready. Read the text around the place you stopped... this is your message from Glinda. How does it resonate with you? How does it apply to you in your current situation or experience?

why the wonderful wisdom of oz?

Why talk about The Wonderful Wizard of Oz?

Because we can understand the infinitely complex through the simplicity of a clever and approachable story. And Oz is a doozy! As you'll soon see, it's the story of the heroic journey of our souls.

The Gift of Allegory

An allegory is a story of deep symbolic meaning, containing multiple symbolisms within it. These symbols represent something real, concrete things and real experiences in your world. Just like *The Wonderful Wizard of Oz*, where Dorothy's journey to and from Oz is an allegory for our own lives. (Oh, just wait you'll see!)

Why do allegories work?

Story telling has been a part of human culture since we first walked on the earth. Our brains are wired to respond to stories. We love listening to stories, love watching them played through movies, and we love learning about someone else's life.

- *Have you ever cried at a movie? Why?* Did you know that person personally?
- *Have you ever watched a thriller movie and physically jumped when the bad guy came out from behind a tree?* Did your heart race?

These are examples of experiencing something through someone else's experience.

You didn't have to know the character in the movie to feel her pain. You didn't have to be running through the dark, scary forest to experience the fear of the character.

We create meaning through stories. They affect how we understand things. And they speak directly to our subconscious mind - while all along we think we are just listening to a story. This is what makes allegories such great learning tools.

They work because they help us take complex concepts and understand them in a way that is simple and approachable. They are easy to remember, give us associations that help us understand, provide frameworks for how we look at things.

The Hero's Journey is an allegory for our human life path, our soul's journey of alchemy and evolution. *The Wonderful Wizard of Oz* is an allegory for each of us as a representation of the journey we are on and the challenges we must be willing to look at and overcome to know ourselves fully... to be fully illuminated... to manifest powerfully and intentionally.

The framework of the heroic journey is a map for us. Ok, I like to call it our yellow brick road. Once you understand it, you can recognize it in any situation or area of your life. Then, you will easily be able to relate it to Oz and lightbulbs will go off for you as you begin to seamlessly and far more easily begin to navigate the creation of your life fulfilled. Cool right?

What is the framework of the heroic journey?

I want you to see the genius of this framework and how it relates to you and how it can help you to gain clarity in any area of your life. The formula of a heroic journey, as articulated by Joseph Campbell, and loosely paraphrased here is:

- ***Part 1*** – our hero/heroine (that's you) is living the status quo, but a conflict arises, and they seek more fulfillment – 'a call to adventure' (sounds familiar doesn't it?); they must leave the comfort of the status quo to accept the call and initially resist. Hey, even Dorothy didn't want to be swept up in the tornado.

  In real life... If you're not living life fulfilled... you may be resisting the call to adventure. In what area of your life are you feeling unfulfilled, thinking about making a change and yet holding on to the status quo, 'for right now'. Perhaps staying in a relationship that is unsatisfying and yet convenient?

- ***Part 2*** – the adventure begins, and our hero meets a mentor or guide and potentially some travel partners who will join them on the journey; obstacles, tests and enemies await them; but they must be overcome together to continue and reach the rewards they desire.

  In real life... you are the hero. Reflect now upon a part 2 of your own heroic journey. A time when you have ventured into unfamiliar territory and found guidance or new acquaintances who have become travel partners. Sounds like just about every new job you've ever had... right? You find a guide, might even be your new boss, and a handful of co-workers with whom you become close and it makes the job more joyful than it would be without them... not without its challenges or tests or drudgeries but, nonetheless enjoyable because of your tribe.

- **Part 3** – the smaller tests have prepared our hero for a life-altering ordeal where their greatest fears are faced (the flying monkeys, silly trees and Wizard, are tests which have prepared Dorothy and her friends for the ordeal of capturing the Witch's broomstick). The reward for facing this ordeal is 'new life'.

  In real life... you may have experienced your part 3 as a difficult conversation with a business partner, spouse/partner, friend, employer, etc.; which resulted in confronting a very difficult situation and perhaps even separation from that partner, position or friend. Hard to face for sure BUT... it left you open for the magic of the Universe to swoop in and deliver your 'new life'. Perhaps a new and better job, relationship, partnership or business!

- **Part 4** – the hero wants to return to 'ordinary', to go back home (Kansas for Dorothy) to the status quo. But, when they return home, they are different, evolved, better. They have been through the fire. They have experienced a metaphorical alchemy.

  In real life... ever returned to a past relationship to give it another try? Returned to a past employer? It felt 'different' didn't it? You returned a more evolved being, maybe having had other experiences or relationships in the absence. Certainly, having faced a few fears and overcome a few obstacles and tests along the way. It feels VERY different. Sometimes you may realize that you've outgrown that other person or employer, other times you may return to find that you are a much better fit this time around.

The allure of the heroic journey is its truth. It's so powerful it is the plot of some of the most recognized stories on earth – *Lord of the Rings*, *Field of Dreams*, *Star Wars*, *Lion King* and of course, *The Wonderful Wizard of Oz*. Every culture has its own set of heroic journey stories.

Unlike the hero's journeys we see on the big screen and experience in books, the one we are experiencing here in 3D, is internal. We do not have to be transported to a foreign land literally, nor slay actual dragons to seek fulfillment and find evolution and 'new life'.

This epic journey is part of being a human. In fact, it's one of the most wonderful things about being human because of how much we learn about ourselves, and through knowing our true selves, we can use our experience to lift others up.

With this book I'm sharing my own experience with the Dorothy allegory (or Oznalogy as I like to call it), the framework it provided which led to deeper self-understanding, and ultimately, represents how I finally clicked my heels and found my way 'home'. And... how you can do the same!

introduction

I'm so glad that the Universe has brought us together. It's not a coincidence that you are picking up this book, in fact as Mike Dooley so eloquently states,

"Accidents, coincidences, and serendipities don't create dreams, your dreams create them."

So, if you are here it is because you are in pursuit of your dreams and the Universe has just given you an intentional coordinate on the path to its achievement. How cool, you're already co-creating!

However, you've not yet living fulfilled, are you?
You are still in pursuit of ultimate freedom – the freedom
to be, do and have all that you desire.

I'll bet that you have read and enjoyed countless self-
improvement books: manifestation books, mindset books,
law of attraction books, spiritual books, make money NOW
books. Perhaps even the wildly popular law of attraction
book, *The Secret*. (It was one of my favorites by the way).

And you've set your intentions on what you desire.
Created a beautiful vision board. Listed and repeated your
affirmations. Set your thoughts to POSITIVE. You might
even have a gratitude journal and a meditation practice!

*But... the glow of anticipation and excitement waned
quickly when you didn't manifest your desires. And then you
felt as if something was missing from those books. Am I
right?*

What was the secret to *The Secret*, the key to
manifestation or the magic spell to money making?

- After all, co-creation is our birthright... right?
- It's easy, "*Ask, believe, receive*" and repeat.
- And yet... you still have not manifested ALL that you
  desire.

Why?

You ARE an infinite being of light, created in the
likeness of our Creator, gifted with the infinite power of

free will and co-creation of your reality. Then why are you somehow unable to co-create the way you desire? Why are you NOT living the life of your dreams?

I have asked myself that very same question. And yet... how can we manifest anything that we desire if we are not willing or able to BE authentic (warts and all, dark and light); to accept, know and activate our infinite potential, to state and feel our intentions clearly to the Universe so that it can deliver opportunities for us to take advantage of and create magic?

Are you saying... wait a second there, Loreen... I AM 'being' authentic, I KNOW I have infinite potential and I've been really clear with the Universe. Oh, *somehow, it's the Universe that doesn't get YOU... is that it?*

The thing is... just a few short years ago, had you asked me, I would have told you I WAS being authentic and being ME and living my passions, speaking out and loving it. In fact, I would have shown you impressive proof! I had manifested my 6,000 sq ft dream house, dream husband, fantastic 6-figure income as an executive in Human Resources that most would only dream of, great company car (a Nissan 350Z called the Blazin' raisin - who doesn't want that?), a cool Mercedes, an awesome Harley, a 2.5 carat nearly flawless diamond ring for my 10th anniversary, 3-week long trips to Hawaii, designer clothes... blah, blah, blah. All the trappings of the Emerald City (but more on that later).

It ALL came crashing down on top of me in 2011 - all GONE. How is that even possible? As a positive person, an infinite being of light AND someone who really 'gets it', a self-proclaimed self-illuminator, where could I have possibly gone wrong? How could that possibly happen?

Please tell me this is resonating with you... have you been there? Thought everything was just peachy only to find out it wasn't true? Is it possible you are headed there now?

Because the thing is... I didn't see it coming. It turns out; I didn't know what I didn't know. And I couldn't SEE what was within me; wasn't willing to face my own shadows and fears and therefore, couldn't truly harness the power of my ruby slippers. It was uniquely hidden, so cleverly by my Ego, to keep me SAFE, to keep me in the hypnotic rhythm of life.

I KNOW you can relate to this. There have been many times in your life that you thought you 'had it together this time' and were on the verge of breakthrough and success and yet... something... just something not quite definable was holding you back. It's just out of your reach - you are searching, you've tried everything you can think of from EFT to hypnosis, meditation to psychics, astrology to numerology and countless other things in between.

So... what is it that you don't know? YOU are the secret, the key, the magic spell and the miracle you seek. IT is within you! You may think you 'know' that but, if you are living life unfulfilled you might want to reconsider.

You see... I thought I 'knew' that but, was living my life successful and completely unfulfilled. Then... I went on a heroic journey to Oz (*you'll learn more about the Wisdom of Oz as we go through the principles*) and finally tapped into my power. Now... I live life FAR MORE fulfilled than ever before. I am more whole, strong, powerful, loving, harmonious and happy then I thought I could be. And... I know you can do the same.

You see... we don't readily see what is within us, because we are in fact, hiding our power from ourselves on purpose to keep ourselves safe. In fact, we often say "*I know that*" and don't examine our beliefs any further because we think we truly do. But what you must realize is this is just a trick of the mind, the Ego; to keep you from having the freedom you desire. If you prefer another perspective, you can see it as the fun game we agree to play here on earth – spiritual amnesia for the purpose of great adventure and growth.

HOW on earth are we supposed to reveal our true gifts, find out what our limiting beliefs are, release them or navigate around them... (yes, that's another cool possibility) so that they no longer have a hold over us and then, shine our light so that we can manifest our dreams?!

Ask yourself honestly right now...

- Do you really know yourself?
- Are you willing to BE yourself... truly?
- Do you know how to 'listen to your heart'?
- Do you take action toward living a life fulfilled, even in the face of uncertainty and discomfort?

You may be thinking at this point... yes, I do... I do know myself and I'm willing to be myself and listen to my heart and I'm moving forward. You might be thinking *"I mean c'mon Loreen, I'm reading your book right now so that's proof I AM doing it!"*

Yet something must be getting crossed in your communication lines... because what you consciously desire is NOT what is manifesting in your physical reality. *Frustrating isn't it?* I know it is, because that is how I felt for far too long.

I know that if you are reading this book it is because you are still growing, evolving, maybe even searching for and seeking 'the answers', 'the way' to create your reality the way that so many self-help gurus have told you is possible!

So, what happened along the way? Why are you not yet where you desire to be? Your unconscious/subconscious beliefs are overriding your conscious desires - just like a bug in the software of life!

But HOW can you get rid of this virus?

Keep reading.... the answer is in Oz.

where is your happy ending?

In *The Wonderful Wizard of Oz,* Dorothy found her way 'home' and got to keep her dream and her dog too. So where is your happy ending and how do you get there?

I guess the first question really should be:

Do you truly want to harness your infinite power?
I'm going to assume your answer is yes since you are reading this book.

Your happy ending begins when you have an honest and truthful NOW. This means getting real with yourself about your current experience. No excuses and no blame. It is only by being completely honest with yourself that you can accurately define the challenge(s) you are up against.

And it must be defined in order to be dealt with. Otherwise you're just hiding behind the Wizard's curtain.

But, hey… it's NOT your fault!

To be honest, one of the reasons we find it difficult to take a REAL authentic look at our NOW is because we've been misled by well-meaning people, and by well-marketed stories which encourage us to think of what we want, believe it will show up and simply wait and draw in our desires. Folks, that's not manifesting, that's simply called dreaming.

Once you've decided you really do want to harness your infinite power, you start with the truth of your NOW.

You are HERE, NOW.

Dorothy was in Kansas with Almira Gulch taking Toto to the Sheriff to be put down; guided by Auntie Em and Uncle Henry, who believe that the power to do anything about it is outside of themselves; surrounded by Huck, Hick and Zeke who talk a big game but conform to their boss's wishes on the farm; finding hope in Professor Marvel who is nothing more than a fake.

You are perhaps in a situation where:

- Your voice is muffled or reduced to a whisper in deafening business speak; groupthink or social norms.

- Your imagination is being squashed, unappreciated or held captive.

- Your thoughts and desires have not yet connected with your courage to take action.

- You're surrounded by people whose passion to shine their lights is dimmed by the lampshades of the corporate offices or the mundane responsibilities of 'life'.

- Your dreams are out of reach pinned on hopes for a lottery win or set aside while chasing the hopes of the next 'get rich using this simple push button' online program, certification or modality.

Where is it you desire to be instead?

Dorothy manifested an elaborate dream to break free from the monotony, the flat unimaginative landscape of Kansas. She desired to be in a colorful, awakened, abundant state of being where her imagination (Toto) would be safe to express itself.

Perhaps you too desire to be in the far more colorful, playful, joyful and prosperous version of your life. A place where your voice is heard and valued, your imagination is set free, you have the courage to take action on your thoughts and desires, surrounded by like-minded and like-hearted beings, knowing what it feels like to be connected to the gold at the end of the rainbow, to be living your dreams in 3D rather than chasing them in 4D (your dreams).

Once you can define your 'I Am Here' (Kansas) and more clearly define the what and why of your 'I Desire to be There' (Over the Rainbow) – then you can begin to see your yellow brick road unfold!

As you take steps on your adventure, along the way you'll begin to uncover the reasons for the obstacles that come with Oz. Find out what has you stuck in Kansas... plagued by the Flying Monkeys in the Dark Forest... Asleep in the Poppies or... pinning your hopes on a Wizard with no powers.

And fortunately for you – you'll have Glinda the good witch (that's me) and *The Ruby Slipper Principles* to guide you from Kansas to Oz to Clicking Your Heels!

Listen... life is like *The Wonderful Wizard of Oz* – it's perfectly reasonable to set sail with nothing more than a dream and a dog (and a great pair of shoes).

tap into your life force!

"The only way to get what you really want, is to know what you really want. And the only way to know what you really want, is to know yourself. And the only way to know yourself, is to be yourself. And the only way to be yourself is to listen to your heart." ~ Mike Dooley

I think that you are here because you know what you really want... but haven't achieved it yet despite everything you've 'tried'. Am I right?

The key to unlocking your infinite potential is within you. You are an incredible infinite being of light. So, the question remains.... *how* do you tap into your life force to release the infinite power of your ruby slippers to manifest anything and everything that you desire?

This is the story of how I went from Kansas to Oz to Glinda. It's the story of my heroic journey from an addiction to silence, to becoming a motivational author and intuitive guide.

How my Kansas kept me small...

When I was around 13 years old, I read Napoleon Hill's "*Think and Grow Rich*" for the first time and unlike other books that I had read, other stories that filled in all the blanks for me... this book left me searching for the answers. From the moment I finished the book, I was hooked on the process. I thought to myself, I'm going to figure this out and then tell everyone else how to do it. I know what I'm meant to do in life... I'm going to be a motivational speaker!

To be fair, my other role models at the time were Anthony Robbins and Mary Lou Retton (Olympic Gold Medalist) and the only way I could wrap my head around sharing this information with others and helping them, was to become a 'success' first and then 'speak' about it to others.

For years I didn't understand how profound that realization would be to me, as I spent my childhood in a state of addiction. Yes, addiction. I was addicted to SILENCE.

There are many forms of addiction and the pattern of addiction would repeat itself in several ways throughout my life. But… that's a topic and discussion for another time. Suffice it to say that the moment in my adulthood when I made this connection, had this understanding, it changed my life!

You see, I grew up in a unique situation. My family was part of a religious cult (*who knew that the Second Coming of Christ lived in the suburbs and drove a Cadillac?!*) I always knew there was something 'not right' about it and that it made our family very different from other 'ordinary' families but, I didn't really understand how it affected me until much, much later in my life.

Not unlike most of you, there are things that impacted us in childhood (Kansas if we're talking about Oz) and have stayed with us through our adulthood and manifest as self-doubt, questioning our worth and lack of confidence to take courageous actions to fulfill our dreams.

Looking back, I can tell you the very moment that my addiction took hold over me. I was 9 years old. I had just finished learning a piece for my piano recital and my mom had promised me that she would buy me the Grease album as a reward.

Maybe not a big deal reward to some but, for me, it was *everything*... you see we didn't have much music in the house outside of show tunes or Simon and Garfunkel or Neil Diamond. All wholesome, good, acceptable music; none of that *crazy radio stuff.* So, Grease, a POP album, was really pushing the envelope, I felt like I'd won the Olympics I was so excited.

As had become the standard daily practice for our family, after my piano lesson my mom and I went to the cult leader's house to visit. I waited anxiously in the front room while my mom visited with 'Him' in the kitchen. I watched the clock... tick, tock... tick, tock... tick, tock... it went from 6:00 to 7:00 to 8:00 to 8:15... 8:30...yikes, I knew I couldn't wait any longer. Kmart closed at 9! How would we get my Grease album if Kmart was already closed?! Clearly my mom had lost track of time again and didn't realize that my long-awaited reward was in jeopardy of NOT manifesting!

So, I did the unthinkable.

I peeked my head around the corner into the kitchen. *"Mom? Can we go now? It's almost 9:00 and Kmart closes at 9. You promised we'd get my Grease album today."*

I don't remember my mother's response. All I know is I had POKED THE BEAR and made 'Him' very angry!

The leader leaned over in his chair and motioned for me with his finger.

"YOU... come over here." (first curling his finger in towards his face, then pointing down to the space directly in front of him.)

Trembling now, I walked over. He seemed larger than life and far more threatening than any Grizzly I could ever meet in the woods. I knew this would not be good.

He towered over me. He looked me directly in the eyes and said in a slow, seething voice, *"Who the hell do you think you are?! How dare you interrupt ME. You are NOT an invited guest in my home, your mother is. I only allow you to be here because she is here. YOU are NOT welcome here, you are a worthless, spoiled brat! You are only allowed to speak if I tell you to speak. If your mother is asked to leave the church it will be all your fault. What do you have to say to that?!"*

An excessive reaction, to be sure.

He rambled on after that... though I don't remember what more was said.

What I *do* remember is going numb, shrinking, cowering and *deciding in that moment...* **I would never speak out again**.

My mother didn't defend me, didn't say a word. Her silence was a sign to me that she agreed with him - that I was worthless and that my voice not only didn't matter, but it could get her kicked out of the church that she loved. I knew in my 'little girl mind' I was a liability to her. My only hope was to stay under the radar, never question authority again and most certainly NEVER ask for anything that I desired or speak up for my own energetic value!

I will never forget that day, that moment, that feeling of intense fear and unworthiness. And yet it would take me years and years to recognize how that moment instantly shifted my beliefs, set invisible boundaries for me and ultimately held me back from realizing my dream of inspiring and motivating others with my voice... for YEARS.

How the experience in Kansas kept me from going over the rainbow

Let's revisit my dream for a moment, what I believed to be my *purpose* in life... how could I possibly achieve my dream and be an inspiring, motivational speaker, if I didn't ever share my voice?

How could I share a message with the world, if I was afraid to SPEAK, to truly honor my authentic being, to believe that I was worthy of a Grease album, let alone infinite freedom.

Enter the tools I did have... what I could do was access my imagination and WRITE. Writing was a safe outlet for my voice; I enjoyed developing and writing stories... that became my release... my way to express myself without giving up my addiction to silence.

The practice of losing myself in as well as *finding* myself in stories is what led me to discover the importance of the heroic journey. We each have one (or more) throughout our lives; but how often do we reflect upon them to capture the gems that they have provided for us?

And... it is what led me to write this book for YOU! THIS is the release of my voice, my gold over the rainbow, it's how I clicked my heels.

Would you explore your heroic journey if you realized it was the key to manifesting everything you desire in life?

That is the foundation for *The Ruby Slipper Principles*. And my hope for you is that you enjoy this EPIC story told with a new 'spiraled up' perspective and begin to appreciate and explore your own heroic journey;

remember, embrace and activate the power of your ruby slippers.

the archetypes of oz

I'm going to take a leap here and assume that you've seen the movie *The Wizard of Oz*, or at least know of the story. Or if you're an over-the-top enthusiast, you probably read the book - or maybe the whole Oz series. (Yes, there was an entire series... 14 books!) At a minimum, you are familiar with the concept because you've picked up this book.

The story of *The Wonderful Wizard of Oz* is great for so many reasons, not the least of which is how it represents the heroine's journey (our internal spiritual evolution) and how each one of us embodies each of the characters (archetypes) in this story as we move through life on our own journey to achieve our dreams.

What are the archetypes of Oz?

Let me begin with the archetypes because they are so central to the understanding of the principles and the Oznalogy (the analogy of Oz which will have you well on your way to understanding how to create a life fulfilled and clicking your heels).

Because Oz is Us, the archetypes in Oz are all aspects of ourselves. Let's take a detailed look at the list of these beloved characters from a new perspective.

This will solidify the language for you and you'll see how these archetypes show up in *The Ruby Slipper Principles* which will be the philosophers stone for your spiritual alchemy.

Dorothy - represents our soul on its physical experience, taking a leap of faith on the heroic journey to spiritual alchemy.

Kansas - represents the physical world we live in, our physical 'home'. It also represents the community of people who we grew up with, our role models, those who shaped and molded us, guided us before we got swept up in our first life altering tornado.

Oz – Kansas is dull and mundane and monotonous – it's a grey and flat landscape. Oz on the other hand is vibrant and joyful and full of intrigue – it represents a higher level of consciousness or state of being, the dream state where we can see our wild imagination speak to us through vivid imagery and tell us rich stories meant to be deciphered into messages we will use when we return to 3D.

The Yellow Brick Road - the path to our illumination, our spiritual evolution and alchemy. Physical alchemy is the transformation of base metals to gold (the color of the yellow brick road), spiritually, it is also known as the 'great work' or the process of transforming the mundane or common into a universal elixir.

The Tornado - People think of the tornado as bad, but it's really the portal from our consciousness to our higher consciousness, in a spiral – a representation of the Fibonacci sequence, as seen in nature, DNA and even in the pattern of the Earth traveling through space. The tornado is like a spiral staircase where we can't see the next steps and must take each step in 'faith'. It is a catalyst to the manifestation of our dreams.

Fibonacci sequence – also known as sacred geometry is a mathematical phenomenon. The ratio of the sequence of numbers (also known as the golden ratio – approx. 1: 1.618) shows up frequently throughout nature in spiral patterns from the branching out of trees, to the spiral of a nautilus shell, is used in art and architecture as an expression of beauty and even shows in the patterns of human DNA.

The Ruby Slippers - represent the Divine spark within each of us - the fire necessary to create the alchemical process. These are the source of your super power!

In the original book the slippers were silver to represent alchemy, remember physical alchemy is turning lead to gold. In the movie the slippers are ruby to represent the philosopher's stone of alchemy. In addition, red is a color that most frequently gets our attention. So much so in fact that STOP signs are red! Red therefore = critically important. Thank you to MGM for that wonderful shift in color and perspective.

Glinda - the Good Witch, represents the Divine Feminine creative energy. She is our higher self.

Munchkins – represent the people, who surround us in a sleep state; who choose to live in the hypnotic rhythm of life. They live within the confines of a cage with an open door yet are unwilling or unable to see how to fly free. They don't even know they are in this sleep state because they are not awake enough to their infinite power and who they really are.

The Wicked Witch - represents our Ego and the hidden aspects of mind control - how we accept the truths we learn outside of ourselves. She is green - the color of money - indicating what we are taught is our source of self-value and what we are to 'love' and desire as representation of success in life.

The Flying Monkeys - represent our limiting beliefs and doubts as well as the false rules meant to keep us in Munchkinland. If you recall from the book, the monkeys were trapped by the spell of the Wicked Witch, the Ego. They are the thoughts and musings of the Ego – the nasty little comments we hear in our head meant to keep us in doubt.

The Rainbow - represents a paradigm shift in our awareness. For Dorothy it is a bridge to Oz and back to Kansas. To us it is a bridge to a higher consciousness and an elevated sense of being.

The Wizard - represents all the false prophets we've followed, all the 'secrets' we've bought into, and our desire to have the 'quick elixir', to believe that there is external magic to completing our internal journey.

The Scarecrow - who doesn't have a brain, represents our thoughts/mind; or more accurately, our lack of awareness of our own thoughts and how they impact our emotions and therefore our actions in the world. The Scarecrow represents our intellectual prowess, our knowledge and our skills.

The Tin man - who doesn't have a heart represents emotions - the emotions we've been holding in, unwilling or unable to express; our burning desire for or passion for our life's purpose. He also represents our capacity for self-love and actualization.

The Lion - who is afraid of his own tail, reminds us of the courage it takes to search for ourselves and to act. *He is the key to manifestation.* We can have the desire and the skills or knowledge to make our dreams come true but without the courage to ACT upon our thoughts and desires, we are just chasing our tails. He is the courage to face our shadow side and that which we fear.

Toto - represents our intuition and imagination. The intuition, a Universal GPS, the hidden force that guides us; the coordinates that seem to be coincidences and synchronicities which keep us 'on track' to our dreams. And, the imagination, the most important human faculty of creation. Did you realize that our imagination IS the gateway to our intuition? Ooh more on that later. No wonder Toto is so key.

The Poppies - represent our addictions - our desire to numb out rather than awaken and face the fire so we can rise as the phoenix. We often succumb to the numbing out the closer we get to our destination.

These Archetypes of Oz and the Oznalogy (which I'll outline for you next) set the foundation of the language that is used in *The Ruby Slipper Principles*. It can now be our own little 'code' of clarity and understanding. And think about it... you'll never again read or watch *The (Wonderful) Wizard of Oz* in the same way... nor see its characters as superficial or just elements of a children's story.

I believe there is comfort in knowing the elements and archetypes of the story and relating them to our current experience. No longer will you hear a fearful thought in your head and just accept it – NO, you will know that it's the Wicked Witch, *the Ego,* sending out her Flying Monkeys, *doubts and fears,* to try to take your Ruby Slippers, *your Divine Spark and true power.*

the oznalogy

Let's take those archetypes and now put them back into their heroic setting. I'd like to share with you what I affectionately call my Oznalogy so that you can see how your heroine's journey is the source of your voice, your passion and your self-discovery; *and* the key to living your life fulfilled. Once you understand the value of your heroine's journey, you will see how you can take a quantum leap toward your dreams with every journey you take.

Before we jump right in to the Oznalogy I'd like to share three quick side notes as I introduce you to the language of *The Ruby Slipper Principles*:

1. **Oznology is the study of Oz, while the Oznalogy is the practice of using the story of Dorothy and Oz as*

an analogy - using the power of the allegory. And yes, it's a word I created 😊.

2. *The term Source is used interchangeably with Universe throughout the book. Source = Universe = Creator = Source Energy = God. Please use the term that most resonates with you or make up your own.*

3. *What is spiritual alchemy?* –While physical alchemy is concerned with turning lead (or other metals) into gold, here we are discussing the spiritual alchemy– a process of illumination, inner liberation a spiritual transformation to freedom.   Here alchemy is expressed as freeing your soul from the lead of false beliefs, illusions, wounds, etc. and transforming into the gold of self-awareness, an unencumbered soul at 'home' – in its divine state of being.

Alchemy in Oz is the act of 'getting out of your own way' to click your heels and find your true being within.

The Original Oznalogy

I call this the 'original' Oznalogy because this is the framework of archetypes and interpretation of the story that was channeled to me way back in 2012-ish when a friend asked me to explain to her why our heroic journey is so important in creating our dreams and sharing our gifts. This, to me, is the beauty of being connected to my intuition because, during meditation this framework arrived like an instant download from the Internet, a realization just came to me... poof... use Oz in this way and move forward. Proof of how the Universe uses any channel to help us achieve fulfillment. I didn't realize the importance of the coordinate at the time but, it would later lead me to this book and so much more!

Let's explore the Oznalogy... the analogy of our experience, a soul's adventure which we can use to learn more about ourselves, our passions, our purpose and our true gifts.

I believe we can all agree that Dorothy is the heroine of this journey but... I'm going to ask you to open your mind and heart to a new interpretation of *The Wonderful Wizard of Oz.*

This story is about Dorothy's transformation, her self-discovery, her spiritual alchemy, the journey to discover her Divine essence. She is searching for herself = 'home' and all the facets of her Self that make her unique and validate her value in this World.

Dorothy believes that she is lost and accesses her deep inner self via a 'dream state' to provide her Self with the allegories and analogies she requires to complete the puzzle and remember her true power.

Our adventure begins when the town 'authority' Almira Gultch wants to have Dorothy's dog Toto euthanized. Feeling that this is terribly unfair Dorothy looks for support from her community, first from the farm hands, Huck, Hank and Zeke and then her Auntie Em and Uncle Henry. Of course, she finds lots of limiting beliefs in Kansas and very little actual help from her support system and her dog is taken by the nasty Ms. Gultch.

Think of a time when you were very excited about a project or business you wanted to launch. Even a fleeting moment when you thought you might want to quit your day job and pursue your passion in life. Who did you go to for support? How did that go for you? Did everyone support you fully and say "Oh yes, go for it! Quit your job today I know you'll be successful!"? Or did their fears and limiting beliefs have them sharing different advice?

Now we have Dorothy's first attempt to leave Kansas as her dog escapes and she decides to run away to save Toto. Of course, she runs into Professor Marvel and looks for one last bit of advice and encouragement for her unconventional plan. Of course, she's met with another disappointment, a person who fears challenging the status quo and guilts Dorothy into returning to her home to care for her Auntie Em whom he tells her (based on his psychic ability) is very ill.

Boy how Kansas has its clutches on us! Let's say your job is a total drain on your joy... what would happen if you just said to your partner, "That's it I'm turning in my 2 weeks' notice tomorrow!"? You might hear some resistance around the bills or the mortgage or maybe even, "hey why don't you just put that off until the car is paid off or the student loan is paid off or until the kids are out of school" ... Welcome the Professor Marvel of your life!

Poor Dorothy, not the answer she was hoping for and now feeling badly, here comes the tornado of confusion and chaos to swoop her up. Equipped with nothing more than a dream and a dog (*her intuition and imagination*) it's too late for her to grab a hold of the cellar doors and stay behind. The Universe has heard her calls to go somewhere over the rainbow and the synchronicity of life is about to make that happen.

These chaotic tornados show up for many of us when we are about to embark on a new spiritual awakening. I like to call it the breakdown before breakthrough. What has been your biggest recent tornado? For me, it was losing my house (hmmm I'm more like Dorothy than I thought)!

She wakes up in Munchkinland, which represents the hypnotic rhythm, the mass consciousness... the 'generally accepted limiting beliefs and thinking of the masses'. The munchkins live in a world of gumdrops and lollipops, afraid to face their fears, but pretending to be or falsely believing they are happy with the status quo.

They will not walk the yellow brick road on their journey to self-awareness but, will happily rely on another outside themselves to deal with the flying monkeys, kill the Wicked Witch for them, freeing them from their own hypnotic rhythm (*their limiting beliefs*) allowing them to have their own Emerald City (*which represents external success/money*).

Now we all know that the Munchkin plan does not work - no one can free you from your fears except you - no one can succeed for you nor can another be responsible for your happiness.

Ever try partnering with someone who comes from a Munchkinland perspective? Say you have a new exciting business venture you propose to a partner, hoping that they would put in shared effort only to be disappointed to find out that they thought YOU would be the one to do all the heavy lifting while they happily take 50% of the big fat check. I know I got the T-Shirt from that trip to Munchkinland!

Glinda, the 'Good Witch' (*representing the Divine Feminine, her Higher Self*) acts as Dorothy's mentor - her spirit guide - her beacon of light. She assists Dorothy in quiet but powerful ways throughout the story. She illuminates the path, the Yellow Brick Road, but, does not and cannot act on Dorothy's behalf - she must allow Dorothy to discover her own strength and power for herself; thereby making her journey that much more transformative.

After her cheerleader Glinda encourages her she can do it, Dorothy sets out to 'find' her powers 'outside' of her self - via the Wizard. You see at this point, Dorothy has no idea she has all she needs within her, like so many of us, she seeks answers outside of herself. In her case, she searches for the Wizard to magically send her home, for many of us we search for the answers in an online program, a job, new certification, a leader/guru who has the answers to our journey. *I know you know what I mean!*

Along the way, Dorothy manifests a life-altering ordeal... she must defeat the Wicked Witch of the West (*a symbol for her Ego - holding her back - keeping her 'separate' from her Oneness*) who holds a vendetta against her. Remember the witch believes that Dorothy is responsible for the death of her sister (the Wicked Witch of the East); and that by birthright, the ruby slippers, worn by her sister and given to Dorothy, rightfully belong to her. (*Ahhh, the frustrating family feuds over the estate of a loved one, need I say more?*).

The ruby slippers represent Dorothy's TRUE powers (*her true identity and entity, her Divine spark of life*) and ultimately can never be destroyed - just as with the Soul. This is why the Wicked Witch covets them so much and will do anything to get them. The Ego fights for its survival - to control the human experience.

The Wicked Witch (*representing the Ego*), uses the flying monkeys as symbols of fears and doubts to keep Dorothy unsure of her path, to distract her from her authentic self. Remember the Witch wants those shoes, she wants the power!

You know that business you wanted to start or service you wanted to provide? The one you were so passionate about. How smoothly has that launch gone? Did you just write the book or program, start practicing the service and put it out there or did you perhaps hold yourself back in the dark forest falsely believing you didn't have what it takes: the knowledge, the skill, the worthiness to earn from your idea; to help others with your service?

Now for our heroine to overcome, she needs support! Because along the way the flying monkeys will keep popping up to deter her from taking another step, to keep her from revealing her truth - her power - her magic.

For support, Dorothy manifests some travel partners with qualities she sees in herself but, perhaps doesn't exhibit fully in her waking life. Her companions are mirrors - they reflect to her qualities she wants to exhibit - who she wants to be. They show up as the three aspects of consciousness, the pillars of manifestation: our thoughts, emotions and actions. In Oz, they appear as the Scarecrow, Tin man and of course the courage to act, the Lion.

Just as we see ourselves in others throughout our lives, Dorothy recognizes these friends at a soul level. They come to her in the form of people she feels very familiar with so that she can trust their powers once revealed (*though physically disguised in Oz, recall they are Huck, Hick and Zeke, the farm hands from Kansas*).

Our authenticity is revealed to others through the transparency of our layers, our depth of wisdom and knowledge; our energy is felt and is familiar to others in our experience - they may not know why they trust us, just as Dorothy doesn't know exactly why she trusts the Lion,

Scarecrow and Tin man but she does - she is comfortable with them because they are a reflection of her.

Each is a like-hearted being on his own heroic journey to find a missing piece of his soul. For the Scarecrow, a brain, to gain the knowledge needed to succeed, to control his own mind. For the Tin man, a heart, to know love truly and to bring passion and purpose to living, rather than being stiff and without animation or desires to succeed. For the Lion, the courage to act, to harness what he thinks and desires into being.

It is said, that we are only as successful as the 5 closest people around us. Who are the folks who comprise your Scarecrow, Tin man, Lion, Toto and Glinda? We tend to stay in the energies of the folks around us – what energy resonance do you find yourself in? Are these people who will walk the Yellow Brick Road with you or do you find yourself surrounded my Munchkins and Wizards?

The Yellow Brick Road (*this is Dorothy's road to enlightenment - her alchemical path*) is her 'bridge' to her answers, to finding her true gifts. At this point, Dorothy believes her destination and answer is with the Wizard; who in her mind is endowed with 'special' powers to magically complete her transformation for her and for her friends. She believes that he can manifest FOR her, that her answers lay outside of herself. (*We've seen this before in Munchkinland haven't we?!*)

Ever wanted to win the lottery? Push a button and have a successful online business? Partner with someone successful, say Oprah and simply have their fans become fans and clients of yours? THIS is simply seeking the riches of the Emerald City and the Wizard's magic. Which, in hindsight we will see, even he does not have!

Not shockingly, before the crew reaches the Emerald City – just short of success – what happens? They fall asleep in the poppies; which represents a moment of self-sabotage as they come close to their perceived goal.

How many of us have done the same? Fear of success, fear of failure, fear of abandonment and poof we're distracted by a shiny object on facebook or the cutest new SnapChat or even a marathon binge session of our favorite new show on Netflix, Hulu, Amazon Prime or whatever. The poppies are where Dorothy and her friends numb out, they avoid continuing the journey if even just temporarily, which mirrors so closely how we progress along our life's journey. Have you ever been really close to the end of a project only to find that you set it aside for a long, long time? Personally, I found myself asleep in the poppies with this book for 6 years!

Finally awake, as Glinda sends a bit of snow, a little inspiration from the Higher Self to encourage them to continue; Dorothy and her friends cross the bridge to the Emerald City. They get one final rejection as the door is slammed in their face – much as the Universe sends us tests of our desires. Almost as if to ask are you CERTAIN you truly desire this? And only when she insists that Source deliver this opening for her do the doors open to allow them in.

Of course, the test of 'worthiness' is not yet over. To meet the Wizard, the team must be 'presentable' – recall that they all had to go to the beauty parlor to get cleaned up, re-stuffed, shined, groomed, etc. One more way that we see how, in real life, emphasis is placed upon outward appearances and influences rather than our internal gifts. We are worthy by birthright, simply by being, yet we often 'dress up' to be seen as something we are not – we are told to *"fake it 'til we make it"* all in an effort to seek the superficial trappings of the Emerald City (*again representing external success and money – a false representation of our true 'value'*).

Finally, they are presented to the Great and Powerful Oz. The Wizard (*ultimately revealed to be a false prophet*) tells her that Dorothy MUST defeat the Witch before becoming 'worthy' of being rewarded her trip back home. She MUST overcome an obstacle (*face her fear, muster up the courage to act*) - get the witch's broom. This act of courage, though unbeknownst to her in the moment, is what will in turn give her permission to feel worthy of her own voice and powers.

We do that too don't we... seek permission outside of ourselves to be who we are and achieve our dreams? Here we can see how desire and thought are not enough to manifest our dreams, we MUST have the courage to act.

Dorothy and Toto in their quest are captured by the flying monkeys (*a team of doubts, all sent to overcome her and her wild imagination, for without imagination we have no creativity and without creativity we have no co-creation of our reality – BIG win for the Witch/Ego*) – and they are taken to the Witch's castle. Of course, Toto (*the human imagination and intuition*) can never be held captive for long, once again escaping.

While Dorothy and Toto have been captured, the Scarecrow, Tin man and the Lion have been left behind in the Dark Forest. It is at this point when we finally see the Lion step up! Though not without fear, he musters up the courage to ACT – to storm the castle in order to save Dorothy! Finally, we can see how desire and thought (Tin man and Scarecrow) are not enough to manifest our dreams, we NEED the courage to ACT.

Dorothy ultimately defeats the Witch. Not intentionally mind you, but in an effort to save her friend the Scarecrow from an untimely death, when the Witch sets him on fire with her broomstick. Once again, Dorothy's success comes almost effortlessly for her (*much as it does for us when things seem to 'magically' align - when we are in resonance with the manifestation of our dreams*). First, when her house landed on the Wicked Witch of the East and this time when the water, meant to save her friend, ends up dissolving the Wicked Witch of the West.

Releasing our own fears and finding freedom is as simple and as difficult as that – for Dorothy she had to use ALL aspects of her consciousness: her mind - the Scarecrow, her passion and desire - the Tin man and the most important of all, her courage to act - the Lion.

Broomstick in hand, she returns to The Emerald City to receive her reward (*and pay-it-forward... receiving rewards for the others as well*). Much to her dismay, upon arrival the Great and Powerful Oz is not pleased and rejects her yet again; asking her to return tomorrow and give him more time to think about it.

Ok so, the heroic journey isn't all gumdrops and lollipops, that's Munchkinland. It's filled with Source asking us over and over and over again to be clear about our intentions and our desires and to take action toward our dreams. Persistence my friend, is key! Even if it's to say NO to the Universe, recalculate that coordinate please and then... push forward.

Ever heard of righteous anger? It's anger that swells within us which is just enough to ignite our courage to ACT. And action is precisely what we need to move forward toward our dreams. Back in the Emerald City, the team is very upset that the Wizard won't keep his promise and Toto, the imagination and intuition which will not be kept still, runs over to the curtain and pulls it back.

Ever had that intuitive 'hunch'? And ignored it? Wished perhaps you hadn't? Recall a time when you honored it, acted and were so grateful that you did?

Here, Toto nudges yet again and this time, Dorothy finally SEES. Alas, it is revealed that the Wizard is no more than a 'man' (*another false prophet*) - an 'ordinary' person - no 'superhero', nothing more special than any of us. Yet he had an inherent, perhaps even subconscious wisdom.

43

He knew that Dorothy had to overcome a great challenge in order to release her fears and achieve her true nature and access her powers.

Sometimes that wisdom comes from the unconscious or subconscious. I don't think the Wizard consciously set Dorothy up to challenge herself as a means to achieving her own power, I believe he had selfish intent – no more Witch to intimidate or control him (just like the Munchkins). That may have arisen subconsciously as a message to him to recognize the rewards that come from facing his own fears.

Dorothy, then becomes a reflection of the Wizard, as he would have had to step out from behind the curtain and reveal his true nature, overcome his own fear of failure and unworthiness to show up authentically in the world.

Unable to truly deliver on his promises, the Wizard gives them each a token of their desires; a diploma, a medal and a symbol of appreciation (the heart clock). The truth of the matter is that at this point they all HAVE that which they desire from within but, as it is for most of us, we still seek permission to be worthy via outside accolades.

How often have you taken another class to become Certified and therefore worthy of say coaching, teaching or becoming a professional practitioner of a service? Attached your value to an external object; a home, car, salary, job title? Asked for a pat on the back from some facebook friends for your latest act of kindness?

Even as the team gets prepared to set Dorothy a sail in the hot air balloon with the Wizard, he pronounces to all of Emerald City that now the Scarecrow, is worthy and to be revered as they would revere him because of his grand intelligence (oh how strong the MIND is, often overtaking our heart and courage). The passing of the torch from one guru to another.

How important is social proof to you? How about the authority of celebrity? Our perceptions are highly influenced by Wizards, smoke and mirrors, and in many cases false claims by marketers and media – all with a hidden agenda which serves an interest which may or may not be for the higher good of all, let alone your own personal greatest good! Remember the Wizard wanted his own freedom and acted selfishly by sending a young girl to fight his battle for him.

As the hot air balloon begins to rise, we see Toto escape yet again! Intuitively, he knows that the Wizard can NOT fly that hot air balloon anymore (seems it's important to use our skills or lose them) and Dorothy may find herself in danger. A final message to heed the warning of your wonderful intuitive nudges!

And that is when Glinda the Good Witch, reveals to her that she has had the power to return home (*know herself*) ALL along. All she need do is remember her truth (*she's wearing the ruby slippers - the Divine Spark – her co-creative powers of manifestation*) and TAKE ACTION... click those heels. And with her fears faced and therefore released, she is FREE to unlock her true gifts and find her way home. Dorothy and her tribe never gave up, they kept moving forward, even in the face of danger and uncertainty and doubt.

Moral of the story: There is no place like home... there is NO greater or more powerful gift than your TRUE SELF.

What can we learn from the 'heroic journey'?

I'm paraphrasing here something I learned from Mark Passio at www.whatonearthishappening.com. Our heroic journey teaches us:

1. to see our physical experience with new eyes, a more elevated and evolved perspective (as Dorothy does in her dream)
2. to seek our 'truth' - true knowledge through discernment (Scarecrow)

3. to develop true care for ourselves, others and this earth (Tin man)

4. to develop the courage to take 'right action' (Lion)

It is interesting to note that Dorothy went on her growth journey in a dream... just as we are able to access our higher conscious (*subconscious*) while we are in a dream state or meditation. In that state, we can bypass our consciousness (our 'monkey mind') and get in touch with our inner being to expand our self-awareness and do self-discovery work. We are able to evolve while we dream or meditate because it helps us to bypass or release our conscious mind to do this kind of work.

Not everyone is ready for the 'Oz' journey... to face the monkeys... to desire to know oneself so deeply that you are willing to go into battle with the Witch. Sometimes it's just much easier to stay asleep in the poppies or live among the fantasies of lollipops and gumdrops in Munchkinland where all appears blissfully happy on the outside.

But each of us can relate to the idea of wanting to know who we truly are; what our purpose is in life, what our unique powers and voice are and to BEING afraid to face our fears to achieve our ultimate dreams.

And though facing the fears is difficult, in the end once we do it, it becomes very easy to release them and their power over us. Remember in Oz, Dorothy simply killed the witch with WATER (*representing our emotions and spirituality*); then the soldiers and monkeys too are set free - for their fears have no power over them anymore!

If Oz (*our dream state*) is the 4th dimension (4D), then as human beings we reveal a bit more of Dorothy every day in our 3rd dimension (3D - *our physical reality*). I believe that every day of 'Oz in 3D' for us serves to help us grow a little more in each role as we reveal more and more the true powers of our own ruby slippers.

Are you beginning to see how spiritual alchemy works?

Through Oz, we turn flying monkeys, dark forests, sneaky wizards and wicked witches from the lead that blocks us and holds us back, into the skills of scarecrows, passions of tin men, and the courage to act like the lions which ultimately sets us free to click our heels home! Alchemy of the soul all found in one little journey - truly proving that you can go anywhere in life with the right pair of shoes!

you are the hero:
the oznalogy of you

"A hero is no braver than an ordinary man, but he is brave five minutes longer." -Ralph Waldo Emerson

What is the heroic journey?

What is the heroic journey? It's an inward as well as an outward journey. It is an internal exploration and adventure to answer the questions... Who am I?... Where do I belong in this world?... What is the key to self-expression - my symbol of identity?... Who do I aspire to become?

AND it's an external experience of action in 3D, to overcome the obstacles and tests along the way via discovery of the power you have always had inside - remembering your gifts, guided by MENTORS, followed by a tribe of like-hearted beings.

A journey you will find yourself on many, many times throughout your life and in a variety of situations. You are always having both a macro and a micro journey simultaneously. The macro journey of self-illumination and soul's alchemy and the micro journeys of everyday life as seen in: your career, hobbies, relationships, finances, health, and so much more.

At the end of every revolution of your macro journey, there is a 'moral' to the story... the line at the end... what you took away as your platform, your mission statement, your manifesto.

Inspired by your own discovery, you share your journey and 'moral' with the world. Thereby inspiring others to take on their own heroic journey and elevating the vibrations of the Earth (big stuff here)!

The heroic journey is a path (our yellow brick road) to help us remember who we are... to help us understand our truest selves as revealed in our story.

Here is how the path reveals itself:

It begins with awareness that we want to change and a desire to be, do and have a different experience.

Point A is NOT where we want to be; it is simply where we are now. Point B - is where we desire to be. That gap in desire creates the tension to journey from point A to point B. When the tension becomes unbearable, (*the desire for point B outweighs the perceived "safety" of point A OR point A becomes too painful for us to remain*) we have a desire to change and finally ACT upon that desire.

Meanwhile in Oz: Toto is sharing his voice and threatened by the mean neighbor, Almira Gulch, who wants him put down; Dorothy wants to let him live. She must decide, is Kansas, with all of its grey landscape and 'traditional' thinking, enough or does she want to expand her experiences, meet new people and allow her imagination to express more freely?

This starts us on a chaotic spiral of change upwards.

Beginning within, often subconsciously, our energy starts to shift with awareness. Many times, I share with my clients that the intelligence of their bodies understands and accepts changes far more quickly than they can consciously. The energy then starts moving forward, elevating, drawing in experiences, situations and people, before we can even comprehend the 'how'. And this is when we feel the chaos begin to swoop us up.

But we don't always recognize the power of our vibrations to attract. We may consciously believe that we only want to attract 'good' things to us - the 'bad' changes must have occurred from outside of us - outside of our control - yet we drew it to ourselves specifically to help rid ourselves of debris that no longer serves us. We begin to change, we alter our vibrations and that which does not serve us is no longer in resonance and begins to fall away as debris.

Meanwhile in Oz: Dorothy runs away to save Toto and seeks guidance from Professor Marvel who tells her that Auntie Em is sick and she must return to her. Now, Dorothy is torn between leaving home to save Toto and staying in Kansas to care for her Auntie Em. But, the energy of change is already swirling about her and in comes the tornado to sweep Dorothy into a new state of being.

We have an "upsetting" experience and land, forever changed by the experience.

We begin to face obstacles and feel a little discombobulated, out of sorts, not ourselves. Yet by just facing the experience, being a part of it, we are now 1 step further along on the journey than another; we've now done something that another has not yet been able or willing to do. Our beacon begins to flicker its light.

Meanwhile in Oz: The tornado lands Dorothy's house on top of the Wicked Witch of the East, altering a part of her Ego forever and giving her a first glimpse at a power she didn't know she had. Of course, the Munchkins are immediately impressed with her 'powers' as she has already done what they could not do.

Much like us, Dorothy doesn't even recognize, let alone value, her 'gift' or her 'power' at this point; because so often things come so naturally to us, that we don't recognize it as 'special' or a 'gift'.

We reach a first obstacle, a milestone and we begin to question our ability, worthiness.

Can we really make this journey? Do we have what it takes? Our Ego flares up, sending messages to stay here, in the hypnotic rhythm where it is 'safe'.

Meanwhile in Oz: The Wicked Witch of the West comes to avenge her sister's life and desires to take the ruby slippers from Dorothy because she knows the power they contain - Dorothy is scared and feels awful about 'killing' the Witch's sister. Which she didn't do 'consciously' and therefore doesn't feel intentionally either. But we're beginning to know better, aren't we? Sometimes our subconscious or unconscious desires set these things in motion as we act, and it is the Universe then that delivers these wonderful (or frightening) coordinates. The fastest path to Dorothy's power was to 'kill' the Witch and get the shoes – so really - that was a 'gift' from the Universe!

Others notice our worth and gifts and believe in us more than we believe in ourselves, encouraging us to keep going for the greater good of all.

Others are inspired by our actions, no matter how small, or insignificant we may feel they are, for we now embody and represent something that we all want; to be, do and have all that we desire, using our passion to fulfill our life's purpose through our gifts! We give them hope that they can be and do the same, if we'll just show them the way.

Meanwhile in Oz: The Munchkins hail Dorothy as their heroine, a good witch, saving them from the wicked witch and... they want more!

The tension to progress on our journey increases.

We feel encouraged and inspired, we have begun to help others by leading the way and have further desire to move forward. Each obstacle we overcome is a 'success', no matter how small we perceive it to be and we begin to believe we can change - we can overcome and are encouraged to go further toward our point B (*our true desire*).

Meanwhile in Oz: Though it's very pretty - Dorothy doesn't want to 'live' in Oz, it feels very foreign to her and she wants to return home. She knows she must do something to continue forward, to find a way home, and the Munchkins are cheering her on.

We seek and find the tools necessary to go further with our journey beginning with a map, a guide.

As we move forward, we begin to see a path unfold, even if just step-by-step. And suddenly, mentors appear to us who have been on a similar journey and can 'light the way' for us. (What's that saying... *"When the student is ready the teacher appears"*?)

Meanwhile in Oz: Glinda notices that Dorothy has begun a journey to harness her inner power and encourages her to go on - showing her a possible path to follow - the yellow brick road. Reminding her that she is protected and that she must keep the protection, her ruby slippers, with her at all times.

Remember that the ruby slippers are the divine spark. That spark of life is our very purpose, the driving fire that gives us hope and the ability to co-create. It protects us on a soul level because it gives us the will to live, to fulfill our soul's destiny and life's purpose.

Our intuition (inner voice) begins to speak up ensuring us we were meant for more in life and have 'enough' to move on.

This is our soul's purpose, driving us toward our goal. The niggling voice within that will have us day dreaming every chance we get, tapping into our intuitive connection through our imagination.

Meanwhile in Oz: Toto willingly follows on the path, letting Dorothy know he will always be there for her and watch out for her – 'alert' her of any danger and support her in going all the way to her dreams.

We begin to elevate our vibrations and attract people and things that help support us in our journey.

Each new individual has something for us - there are no coincidences, we meet everyone for a reason, each is a mirror with a message, a new light, a new glimmer of our self-illumination, a piece of the puzzle that guides us closer to our point B.

Meanwhile in Oz: Dorothy finds others who are also on a journey of self-illumination, Scarecrow, Tin man and Lion, who have also felt the tension to be more, are willing to walk with her.

Another obstacle/milestone, fear arises, we question if we are worthy enough.

Along the journey we are challenged, fears arise and we self-sabotage, questioning if we can indeed make the journey. Our Ego consistently seeks to drive the process, to keep us safe, and our false/limiting beliefs emerge to block our infinite power.

Meanwhile in Oz: The Wicked Witch sends out her flying monkeys along the yellow brick road to try to stop Dorothy – to capture her dog (*her imagination and intuition, her alert system*), to harm her friends (*her thoughts, desires and will to act*).

We are tempted to succumb to the Ego, we may even STOP our journey - stay back in the hypnotic rhythm for a period of time.

Feeling it is so much easier to simply stay where we are than it is to forge ahead, often stopping just "*3 feet from gold*," as Napoleon Hill would say. It is so much easier to numb out or avoid than it is to face our fears, even when that fear is the fear of success.

Meanwhile in Oz: The Witch casts a spell so that the poppies put Dorothy and her friends to sleep in the field just before they reach the Emerald City.

We seek answers/help outside of ourselves.

Believing we need more help, in the form of education, skills, guidance, experience before we can be worthy of achieving our dreams. How many times have you simply ordered another book, course or program rather than launch your own gifts to the world 'as is'?!

Meanwhile in Oz - Dorothy and her crew know if they can just make it to the Emerald City, the Wizard will perform his magic and give them what they each desire.

We are faced with the ultimate challenge, we must slay the dragon to take the castle and have our dream come true.

We manufacture a way to prove our own worth of our ultimate desire. This is what is called our Chiron in astrology (named after the centaur in Greek mythology), the wound we have come to 'heal' in this lifetime. And yes, we really do draw these things to ourselves; we set them up in advance, as contracts or agreements with our Soul for this journey to Earth (or is it Oz?).

Have you noticed that certain patterns show up in your life over and over and over again? It could be in love, business, finances, relationships, but it shows up to ask you yet again to face it, learn from it, act to dissolve it and then elevate beyond it to see it from a new perspective. Now you are beginning to peek at your soul's purpose.

Meanwhile in Oz: The Wizard does not award Dorothy and her friends their desires on their first trip to Emerald City, instead he tells her she must get the Witch's broomstick to be worthy of his rewards - she must ultimately take control of her Ego and recognize her infinite power within (*her truth*) as greater than the Ego.

We reach and overcome the final milestone.

We prove to ourselves that we are worthy of allowing our ultimate desires. Most often overcoming that milestone is as simple and challenging as facing our fear, the limiting beliefs we have adopted, the stories we've been telling ourselves; recognizing it, accepting that it has been with us and then releasing it through forgiveness. And once we do, it simply dissolves and is no longer an obstacle or deterrent to us.

Meanwhile in Oz: Dorothy pours water on the Wicked Witch, freeing her soldiers, and her friends to return to the Emerald City with the broomstick to receive their rewards.

Abundance is ours. We reach the gold at the end of the rainbow!

Having overcome each milestone, we reach our desired destiny. Though our gold isn't always as we thought it would be when we began at point A... e.g. some of us begin seeking money when what we truly desire is freedom, to be able to fly free; no longer a bird in a cage with an open door.

Meanwhile in Oz: Dorothy goes back to the Emerald City to accept her 'gold', her rewards, and the

Wizard, it is revealed, is nothing more than a man... and simply hands out to each of her friends mere symbols of their actual desires: a degree instead of a brain, a medal of bravery rather than courage, a clock in the shape of a heart rather than an actual capacity to love, and for Dorothy a realization that no certificate, medal or heart will be enough to carry her back to Kansas.

The ah-ha moment - the epiphany - it all comes together.

This is the moment when we have our own 'peek behind the curtain' - what was once hidden and seemed beyond our reach because it was outside of our perceived self-value or ability is accepted as not only possible but probable. We connect all the dots and, in a blink, just 'get it'. Ahhh. Finally! Am I right?

Meanwhile in Oz: when it is revealed that the Wizard is nothing more than a common man, Dorothy is a bit confused and disappointed but alas, she retains hope because he has a hot air balloon and says he will take her back to Kansas.

Now Glinda helps to guide her to her ah-ha moment. Toto realizes the Wizard can't fly the balloon (he jumps out knowing Dorothy will go after him) and Glinda helps her to remember she must rely on herself, for she has everything she needs to be her own Wizard, to control her own destiny within her already... she simply needed to REMEMBER her heroic journey as it unfolded to remember her true infinite power.

We leave the heroic journey a changed person with a message for the world - the moral of our story is...

We take away from the experience a new perspective on life... and we now have the ability to take a very complex concept, a very rich experience and express concisely what we have learned and what we now 'stand for' as the hero or heroine. We have a message to share with the world. Woohoo – we've found our VOICE!

Meanwhile in Oz: the moral of the story is "*there is no place like home*" - there is no greater more powerful gift than your authenticity - your self - your true power - your voice.

We are all one, we are always home, there is no separation, we are each infinite beings of light with the power within us and straying from that is simply an illusion of separation which causes fear, uncertainty, and questioning our value.

We feel inspired to share our message with the world.

We have a responsibility, a desire to share this with the world - it is our 'life's purpose' it is what drives us from the beginning of our experience asking, "Who am I?", "Why am I here?" "How do I get to where I desire to be?"

Now... having felt success, experiencing the ah-ha moment and knowing we can never return to the 'old way' of being or thinking... we are inspired to share this wisdom with others so that they too can feel our joy and live more fully in this life. This is what I call *'passion-it-forward'*. The way we express love for humanity is to share our gifts with the world.

It is every soul's purpose to grow, evolve and learn through simply authentically BEING and experiencing the adventure of life through the path of our desires. This in turn inspires others to do and be the same and elevates the vibration of the energy of the Universe.

Our life's purpose (slightly different than our soul's purpose) is to serve others through the expression of our soul's purpose. Again, we elevate the consciousness of the globe by sharing our gifts and wisdom. Our heroic journey is the culmination of BOTH – our soul's purpose to go for the gold over the rainbow and our life's purpose to bring it home to share with others.

Meanwhile in Oz: Dorothy upon finding herself back in Kansas is so excited to share the experience with her friends and family she can hardly contain herself and must tell them what she has 'learned' and 'gained' having been a part of the experience. It is her way to express love and to inspire (to breathe life into) others.

We are each here on a journey to reveal ourselves, to remember our Divinity, and we can do that through our own heroic journey, walking our own yellow brick road and helping our friends along the way.

Each of *The Ruby Slipper Principles* will take you through an element of your own experience, your own heroic journey, from the most chaotic storm of your tornado all the way through to your own ah-ha moment - the moment you recognize your unique inner power, your ruby slippers, and you click your heels, inspired to share the moral of your story with the world in an exciting new way.

the ruby slipper principles: a hot air balloon perspective

The Action/Adventure Guide Begins Here...

The 12 principles to help you navigate your heroic journey; overcome self-doubt, stop questioning your worth and start taking courageous action toward creating a life fulfilled. Ready?

Using the Oznalogy and our new archetypes for Oz, you'll find that the Ruby Slipper Principles are the principles by which you can navigate your heroic journey. Using them, you will easily be able to identify where you are on your own journey to Oz; and you'll be able to frame your experience within the Principles, recognizing both what you have achieved to that point and what is yet up ahead for you as you evolve.

Let's turn personal development and self-discovery upside down for a new perspective that is both illuminating and approachable.

Hot Air Balloon look at the 12 Principles

Let's look at the 12 Principles from a 'hot air balloon' perspective. Then we'll go down to Oz level and really start putting those feet to the yellow brick road as it were.

1. ***You're Not of Kansas Any More*** – you haven't quite realized your dream.

   Why? Kansas is for Auntie Em and there is no Ruby Slipper store there. You may be IN Kansas, but you realize you are not *of* it anymore.

2. ***Feed Toto*** - because when you nurture your intuition and imagination, you honor the most important faculty available to the human soul.

   You're well on your way. Watch for alerts, because on your adventure you will receive coordinates from your Universal GPS but, may not recognize them or take inspired action unless you are 'tuned-in'.

3. ***Embrace the Tornado*** – it leads to great adventures and growth.

The chaos you feel when you begin the next revolution of your evolution is the Universe's way to say, "*I hear you. Let's get you OUT of Kansas and on your way to Oz.*"

4. **Call on Glinda** - because good witches stick together and help one another navigate the yellow brick road of life.

     At this point in your journey you have great tension to move forward despite your fears, to find your yellow brick road, to get on the journey to finally click your heels. It's time to establish lines of communication with your Higher Self.

5. **Break Free from Munchkinland** - the hypnotic rhythm of gumdrops and lollipops is not soul nourishing.

     You have likely been a Munchkin in your past; and admired the bravery, courage and success of another; longing to be 'in their shoes'. Here's your chance at your harmonic rhythm! You have just left the cellar seekers behind and earned your ruby slippers.

6. **Follow Your Yellow Brick Road** – it leads to profound spiritual and life alchemy.

     You've got the shoes, you've got the desire, and now all you need is a path. Not just any path,

YOUR path to your true self, the one that guides your soul's purpose. If you desire it, you'll know and there you'll go. You can NOT take a wrong step if you are stepping in the intention of your yellow brick road.

7. ***Introduce your Intellect and Heart to your Courage*** - they are the 3 pillars of manifestation. Elevate your company and elevate your experience.

Time to lock arms with your allies to higher consciousness and manifestation! Just as Dorothy had friends to journey with her, so shall you. In fact, they are likely all around you all the time and you just do not recognize them for the gifts they bring you.

8. ***Defeat the Flying Monkeys*** - fears and limiting beliefs serve only to send you back into Munchkinland.

Along the way to your desires, you will encounter societal norms, fervent religions, and media messages, developed to control you through fear. The Witch truly hopes that her advertising is working on you and soon enough you'll turn your slippers over to her. But you know better, don't you?

9. **Stay Awake in the Poppies** - avoidance will not get you to the Emerald City.

   The Emerald City is very close now, you're almost there! The stronger the pull to sleep, the closer you are. Now is the time to tap into Glinda and ask for help. Brrrr I feel the snow falling.

10. **Peek Behind the Wizard's Curtain** - the answers are not in false prophets or illusions of worth.

    You are worthy by birthright, equipped with all the necessary pillars of manifestation but, in order to reveal them you must go within and connect to your intuition.

11. **Pour Water on the Witch** - her desire is mind control, yours is freedom.

    The time has come to face your fears, release your limiting beliefs and free yourself. Remember there is no manifestation without inspired, courageous action.

12. **Click Your Heels** – harness your infinite powers to manifest your desires.

    This is it! You've landed in Oz. You have been awarded a pair of ruby slippers and it is your soul's purpose to click them and find your way home.

ruby slipper principle 1:
you're not of kansas any more

You're Not of Kansas Anymore

You haven't quite realized your dream. Why? Because, Kansas is for Auntie Em and there is no Ruby Slipper store there. You may be IN Kansas, but you realize you are not of it anymore.

You are here.

Where is Dorothy when she starts? She is in Kansas, frustrated because Almira Gulch, a rich, arrogant woman, wants to kill her beloved dog Toto, her soul, her connection to the Divine, her desire to be free. A force outside of her wants to control and oppress her experience, to limit her freedom.

Perhaps you can relate? Where are you now? We have already established that you've not yet achieved all that you desire in life. You have not quite realized your happy ending, at least not for this phase of the journey. Why is that? It's because...you are in Kansas and there's no ruby slipper store!   For that you must go on a heroic journey.

Let's assume for a minute then that your dream is to harness the infinite power of your ruby slippers (to fulfill your soul's purpose, passion and joy). And let's just say that your dream falls just outside the conventional traditions of a job and a house and a family, etc. Where do you go for help in achieving your dream?

Let's go back to Dorothy's situation, when she wants to defend Toto, she seeks approval from trusted sources. She goes to her Auntie Em and Uncle Henry to plea for their understanding and to each of her friends on the farm, Hick (the Tin man), Huck (the Scarecrow) and Zeke (the Lion). She does her best to awaken them and yet she is met with resistance and the 'common thinking' of well-meaning folks who are not yet awakened. While they appreciate her being unhappy with the situation, they seek to offer her advice which will keep her within their illusions of safety.

What is the illusion of safety?

The illusion of safety is thinking that the well-meaning beliefs we've adopted from our role models, are in our soul's best interest. We come to this journey pure and whole and infinite in our potential. As we grow, we are 'guided' by those around us. Soon we begin to form our beliefs and our truths based upon what we've been told or what we've experienced. We adopt those beliefs nearly seamlessly and incorporate them into our state of being. Those beliefs establish our boundaries, our limitations. Anything outside of those boundaries or beliefs then feel uncertain to us and therefore 'unsafe'.

For Dorothy, when her dog Toto is threatened, she is faced with the 'illusions' and boundaries of her family and friends. Let's see how this played out...

Auntie Em and Uncle Henry make her turn Toto over to Miss Gulch – they have learned NOT to question authority and have accepted that the rich folks in the neighborhood can get whatever they want, despite being deceitful to get it.

Huck (the Scarecrow) tells her to "think it through", to avoid the conflict by not going anywhere near Miss Gulch's garden on her way home. He has adopted a belief that if we are smart enough, if we put our mind to it, we can solve the problem by avoiding it or finding a way around it.

Hickory (the Tin man) tells her to "have a heart", take pity on Miss Gulch who is a lonely, unhappy woman. He has adopted a belief that we should put others before ourselves.

Zeke (the Lion) tells her to "have some courage", confront her and *"spit in her eye"*, a pretty bold statement to fight fire with fire. He has adopted the belief that we must FIGHT for what we want.

Know this now, if you have not yet fulfilled your purpose...
It's NOT your fault!

We are conditioned when we are very young to listen to the guidance of our role models, our mothers, fathers, teachers and spiritual guides. But often they have already succumbed to the boundaries and beliefs of those who shaped them; it is a cycle which continues through generations. Until... we decide that we're NOT to be in Kansas anymore!

Think about how these beliefs may have manifested in your life and kept you in Kansas. Perhaps you believe that you need a degree to be successful; or that you must put others in front of yourself in order to be worthy of love; or that you must always resist change; *"we've always done it this way", "don't fix what's not broken".* Perhaps you've not pursued your dream because it's unconventional or not *"what people do to earn a decent living"*, or you've learned that only the rich get ahead because it takes money to make money. All of these are examples of the 'illusions of safety'.

What messages have you adopted from Kansas?

Whatever your beliefs and boundaries, when you recognize them holding you back and your desire to click your heels is stronger than your desire to stay 'safe'; this is where the struggle/conflict begins, the fight between the ego and the soul. The ego seeks to keep us 'safe' feeling bound by our beliefs and conventions. The ego seeks to maintain power and keep us bound to our current illusions; this is how it ultimately survives. The soul, however, seeks to fly, to live out its true purpose, to be free.

Recall that the Ego in the Oznalogy, is represented by the Wicked Witch of the West, who first rears her ugly head in Kansas (as Almira Gultch) when she seeks to destroy Toto. Toto, representing the human intuition and imagination, is the true power of any individual/soul to break free. Can you see how imagination (Toto) - the human soul's most important faculty - is a threat to the Witch, the Ego, who seeks to control the soul and only exists on the human plane?

For Dorothy, she recognizes that Kansas and her current support system are NOT aligned with where she desires to be. At this point she begins to question her identity and begs to ask the question: "*If not here, who and where do I desire to be?*" In her heart she knows that she desires to be somewhere over the rainbow.

This is the phase during which we begin our transformation. Dorothy begins searching for her SELF - her 'home' - all the facets of her Self that make her unique and validate her value in this World. She has asked the Universe for her ruby slippers by the pure nature of recognizing that she's IN but not OF Kansas anymore.

ENTER assistance from Source. Her expectations no longer match her expectancy and the winds of change begin to swirl!

You are her... excited about your dreams but met with feigned enthusiasm or worse the fears of others who wish to keep you 'safe' by encouraging you to stay within the current boundaries. Whatever those boundaries may be for you or for them I would encourage you to examine them and ask yourself if they are working for you or if you might be better off leaving them in Kansas.

Now click your heels here to go over the rainbow...

Let's look at the 5 major things you'll need to go over the rainbow and click your heels to dreams fulfilled: your intuition (Toto), your knowledge (Scarecrow), your passion/desire (Tin man), your courage to act (Lion) and your co-creative power (ruby slippers).

Are you in Kansas but not of it?

What do you BELIEVE about the following areas of your life?

Intuition: Are you intuitive? Psychic? Can you be? Why?

Knowledge: Do you have the skills and knowledge you need to live your life fulfilled? What, if anything, do you need to know before you can achieve your dreams? Do you doubt yourself? Why?

Desire: Do you know your soul's purpose? What are your gifts? Your passions? Are they valuable? Are you valuable?

Courage: Do you act in the face of fear, despite discomfort? Have self-confidence?

Co-creative Power: Are you a powerful being? Who are you? Why are you here? Can you create a magical life?

Now review your answers and ask yourself:

Where did that belief come from? Is it perhaps a belief you adopted from Kansas? Can you remember hearing it as a child? From whom?

Is that belief serving you now? Is it helping you to achieve your dreams... to create a more fulfilling life?

In what way are you no longer "of" Kansas even if you find yourself still in it?

---

ruby slipper principle 2:
feed toto

Feed Toto

When you nurture your intuition and imagination you honor the most important faculty available to the human soul. And, you honor your most important co-creative super power! Looking for clarity and direction? Watch for alerts now, because along the yellow brick road you will receive coordinates from your Universal GPS but, may not recognize them or take inspired action unless you are "tuned-in" to your best friend Toto.

Looking for clarity and direction?

Our intuition/imagination is the most important faculty available to the human soul - it will NOT be contained it will always seek freedom – just as Toto always escapes the clutches of the Witch (and Almira Gulch when they are still in Kansas) and he jumps out of the hot air balloon that the Wizard is driving, knowing it would not ultimately get Dorothy home safely.

Likewise, the intuition will not be made a fool, just as Toto pulls back the curtain on the Wizard. Our intuition is loyal, unconditionally loving and always has our best interest at heart, as dedicated to us as Toto is to Dorothy, as any dog we have in our lives as companions. So, we must care for it as we would our most cherished pet.

Why do you think that the Witch so fiercely went after Toto?

The Ego seeks to capture the imagination because the imagination is the gateway to the intuition. It is how we communicate with the Divine. How we get our Universal GPS coordinates for our voyage; our co-pilot in clarity.

Without this connection we wander aimlessly in circles, returning to Munchkinland and settling for the hypnotic rhythm of life. How easily we tend to dismiss our imagination as nothing more than silliness, yet had Dorothy ignored Toto she'd not have revealed the false promises of the Wizard.

Surely, you've said to yourself on more than one occasion-

"Wish I'd trusted my gut on that one!"

When we keep the channels of Divine communication open, we are always guided along our path, toward our truth and the revelation of those wonderful synchronicities which open new doors of opportunity for growth and prosperity for us. Now co-creation is becoming clearer and getting more interesting isn't it? No wonder the Witch wanted this super power!

Toto is key to manifesting your fulfilled life and throughout this book you'll be asked to tune into your intuition and imagination which will serve as your Universal GPS, a powerful navigation tool.

How to best nurture your intuition ···

Feed Toto

Our intuition, like Toto, though unconditionally supportive, does require care and nurturing. Everyday our pets need food and water, shelter from the elements.

Nurture your intuition as you would Toto. Feed your intuition with wonderful wisdom, give it something to chew on, ask it questions, and seek guidance from it every day. Give it opportunities to feed information and insights back to you as it becomes fuller when it knows it has served you.

Protect Toto

Just as you put a leash on Toto so that he won't be stolen by Almira Gulch and you release that leash once he's safe and sound in his bed in your home, take care to honor and protect your intuition.

Protect your energy throughout the day. This can be as simple as pulling your aura in closer to you for the day to protect it or you may have a protective symbol or talisman that you like to use or a crystal.

Likewise, at the end of the day, clear out any toxic energy in your field, cut any energetic cords that may have become attached throughout your day. Again, this can be as simple as unhooking the leash from Toto, you might simply ask for your Higher Self to come and spend a moment with you to sever the energetic cords that have become tied to you for the day.

Greet Toto

Connect to your intuition every day. You wouldn't come home from work and ignore Toto, would you? No, you'd greet him at the door, and he you, with a wagging tail and anticipation of your time together.

Your intuition awaits you every day and joyfully accepts the time you connect. Much like dogs, our intuition does not require much to be happy – a very simple greeting will do. Take a moment to be present every day and to notice the signs that your intuition is sending you. See a feather, a favorite number, hear a song you love, say "*Oh hi, there you are!*" When you say hello to your intuition or use your imagination, you recognize that the two of you are connected. All you need do is to BE PRESENT. C'mon let them sit on your lap as you relax at the end of the day or at least sit at your feet.

Take Toto for a Walk

Toto, like so many other dogs is curious and highly intelligent and needs to explore in order not to become restless. For dogs, going for a walk is like reading the news feed, it has all kinds of intriguing information that stretches their mind, and feeds their curiosity. Take your intuition for walks!

Stretch your intuition, play with your imagination, give it a chance to explore new avenues, connect through meditation, try divination using tarot or oracle cards, spend some time writing in your journal, just allowing the words to show up for you. Create the space for your intuition to express itself, give it a chance to draw in new information and expand its reach. You may feel tired at the end of the session but, you'll have an entirely new route you are familiar with and it makes the normal 'routine' that may have become static, feel exciting and new again.

Play Fetch with Toto

Most dogs LOVE to play, they are full of joy! Just like you would play fetch with Toto for fun... play fetch with your intuition.

Be light-hearted with your intuition, ask for guidance and then ask for it to show you the answers through signs or to give you information in a new way. Toss out your question and then be present for the answer to return to you in a new way. Perhaps you'll start noticing animals come into your experience or numbers will pop out at you, perhaps you'll see signs on the road or passages in books will suddenly profoundly impact you.

Be present and patient. Ever toss the ball for your dog and then walk away? Did they come find you? Bring that ball in the house; drop it at your feet? Fetch with intuition may not be as immediate as fetch with a dog but, your answer will be returned to you and your intuition will NEVER grow tired of the game.

Pay Attention to Toto

Dogs bark (and howl)! And when they do, they are usually trying to voice something; they may want your attention because they need to go out or they may sense that there is a threat and you need to be protected. Admittedly sometimes they'll just nudge you, pull at you or place their paw on you. When your intuition nudges you... pay attention. Toto was the one to pull back the curtain and expose the Wizard as nothing more than an ordinary man.

How does your intuition nudge you? Pay attention to the senses in your physical being, be it messages you hear, feel, taste, see or think. Get to know your intuition's language... is it barking at you (usually easiest to notice), growling, whining, nudging, or just pawing?

Just as with dogs, our intuition has its own unique language and it is always trying to communicate with us to serve our higher good. We learn how our dogs communicate via their patterns and repetition; you will learn the language of your intuition the same way. Be patient and present and it will reveal itself as a useful resource.

The language of your intuition

To illustrate this further, let's look at the different ways in which our intuition uses different types of language. We all have different clairs or psychic senses. You may have more than one language of your senses but are likely dominant in one and supported by the others. The primary clairs are as follows (there are others that are present but less common such as clear scent or taste, which we will place under clairsentient for purposes of this book):

Clairvoyant (see) – you have clear vision or perceive things with the mind's eye. You receive your messages from Toto through your visions.

Clairaudience (hear) – you have clear hearing or perceive your messages through sound. You may then hear Toto barking, like whispers in your ear.

Clairsentient (feel) – you have clear feeling or perceive information through touch or sensations in the body. You may receive message from Toto as a 'pit in your gut', 'strong winds blowing'.

Claircognizant (know) – you have a clear knowing or perceive information through your thoughts. Toto may message you by giving you a piece of information which just shows up in your thoughts and you don't know where it came from.

- If this is your predominant clair, *and you will likely have more than one*, it may often feel like you're just 'making things up' when they POP into your head or your space of 'knowing'. More than the other clairs, it will be critical for you to trust and follow your IMAGINATION because it is truly the door to your intuition. If you 'think' it or it just 'comes to you' – SPEAK it or write it down no matter how foolish you might feel about it. This is great practice in building trust with this channel.

Now you are more aware of the language of your faithful friend. So, be present and alert so that if Toto wants to communicate with you, you will notice the signs appearing in your thoughts, visions, sounds, and feelings.

All you must do to take advantage of this wonderful superpower that you have is to be present to it. When you are alert and in sync with your intuition, you will receive coordinates from your Universal GPS. However, you may not recognize them or take inspired action unless you are 'tuned-in'. Don't stay asleep in those poppies!

How can Toto help you overcome self-doubt?

Let's talk about self-doubt for just one moment. How often have you felt unclear... uncertain... in the dark about the direction you should take... the decision you should make... the clients or even friends you should allow in to your life?! How often have you maybe 'prayed' for direction or an answer or asked for your angels or guides to just please send you a sign?!

All that uncertainty leads to self-doubt. And that self-doubt leads us to procrastinate and to go down the rabbit hole of further education, or courses or coaches or friend's advice to help us gain clarity; rather than take action toward our fulfilled life!

How might your life be different if you had more CLARITY? Would you doubt yourself less? I'll bet you would. And who can come to the rescue and give you the clarity you so desire? Toto! (Ok, by Toto I truly mean your intuition.) When you have a relationship with your intuition and you practice tuning in to its frequency, you can have far more clarity and remove that dreaded self-doubt monkey! Cool right?

Your intuition can provide you with signs, signals, feelings, thoughts and messages that reveal the best direction for you in the moment. Real clarity! It's at your fingertips, with you always, all you need to do is FEED it, pay attention to it, nurture it.

Now click your heels here to connect with Toto, you'll need him for the adventure...

connect now

Take a moment to connect now.

First, be aware of which breed your intuition is. Which Clair is your most predominant/2nd most predominant?

Next, take a moment to set the intention for the area of your life in which you would like some guidance or clarity.

Now, be alert to the signs, symbols, feelings, messages, and thoughts that come to you throughout the day as you walk your yellow brick road. Jot down anything that arises for you. Keeping a journal of your intuitive alerts will show you how a yellow brick road is unfolding for you to follow.

Notice, what happens when you act upon the signs you receive and what happens when you don't.

ruby slipper principle 3: embrace your tornado

Embrace your Tornado

The chaos you feel when you begin the next revolution of your evolution is the Universe's way to say, "I hear you" let's get you OUT of Kansas and on your way to Oz.

Your journey begins.

When you are asking the universe for ruby slippers, to be able to click your heels and manifest whatever you desire; Universe says OK, there are things you need to change that you haven't yet. So, to truly manifest what you desire I will sweep you up in the tornado to help you get to where you are going. But... fair warning... you cannot control it.

It will take you from a situation where you are trying to control everything, what and how it happens, to a situation where you have absolutely no control; because it is the path that allows the Universe the freedom to present you with the synchronicity and coincidences to achieve your dreams.

And... you probably need to recognize at this point, as I do with every succeeding tornado, that you're not well suited for the job of Director of the Universe, it does nothing more than keep you in Kansas!

Recall in *The Wonderful Wizard of Oz*, just as Dorothy sets out to face the challenge, share her voice and save Toto from certain death - she is swept up in the tornado. This tornado is the chaos we frequently feel when we are beginning a new phase in our evolving journey.

What makes the hero heroic is the one who can embrace being uncomfortable.

To be able to say - I'm in the middle of a tornado – I don't know what will happen to me - I'm afraid. But I'm going to allow this tornado to sweep me up anyway. That is heroic!

If we allow it to take us and be in that space, it will literally transport us on a whole new journey.

Let's be honest here and say that what most of us would rather be doing is hiding with the cellar seekers (they keep wine in cellars, right?). We will do nearly anything to avoid being uncomfortable – to keep the tornado away. We don't want to look at finances... don't want to end the bad relationship... don't want to have that difficult conversation. We have said to ourselves, *I'm just going to wait out the storm. It will go away... or calm down.*

However, if Dorothy had found her way to the cellar, she never would have taken the tornado, wouldn't have be transported to Oz. She wouldn't have the epiphany moment of the house falling on the witch and leaving behind the ruby slippers for her. She would not have become the heroine if she hadn't gone through the tornado. True enlightening and dream fulfilling spirit is embracing the next tornado because it opens you to a whole new world you wouldn't see if you stayed in the cellar crunching numbers, planning direct routes or accepting the boundaries and fears of others.

How do you embrace tornado without being torn apart by it?

To embrace the tornado, first you must TRUST the tornado. The tornado is the symbol of our connection, the tunnel between earth and spiritual sky... a divine channel; a portal between lower and higher consciousness.

The shape of the spiral, our DNA, the expression of the mathematical Fibonacci sequence, is how the Universe evolves. Think of the tornado as the Universal cornucopia in reverse, we are the source, the point of origin and meant to SPIT out our abundance to the Universe. As we elevate our energy - spiral UP and OUT - we grow wider with our perspectives and we offer MORE enlightened energy to the Universe - our gift back.

Trusting in that divine channel will allow you to let the debris fly around you without trying to fight it or engage it. Use the energy of the spiral to brush the old out of your energy field and propel you forward. Letting it go puts you in a place of ease and flow. Now, when I say brush the old out... what I mean is energetically. You don't have to stop loving the people in your life, don't have to physically give away your stuff, simply 'detach' from it – cut the energetic cords that are binding you so that you can see those relationships, things, situations transform – make sense?

It's only in our resistance of the tornado that we get torn apart by it.

When we are ruined by a tornado is when we wanted to be in the cellar door but didn't quite make it; holding on to old beliefs, old ways of being that are no longer assisting us in our evolution.

In the chaotic moments, things will fall away; it's our choice how to respond to it. Sometimes the debris that is cast off is neither what we expected nor what we desire. For instance, we may see partnerships dissolve, houses foreclosed on by the banks, jobs lost. When we try to hold on to the debris, that's when we're torn apart. Debris that no longer serves us is being eliminated from our lives - so that we CAN'T hold on to it any longer.

Remember you asked for the ruby slippers, your dream fulfilled, this is the Universe helping you to get what you want!

Feels strange and disorienting doesn't it?

Our fear is always that the tornado will kill us. But if we're in the eye of the storm, eventually it spits us out. By the time Dorothy lands, she's had her first success. Her willingness to embrace the chaos lands her on her first witch – the decision to leave Kansas was a good one and she is rewarded with the ruby slippers!

Your first success within your journey is the willingness to sit with that uncomfortableness, the chaos of the tornado. You too will land and find that you have made a huge leap in your progress, and you will have earned those ruby slippers!

This is why the 3rd principle is to embrace it; accept the tornado has come to you to propel you further on your heroic journey. You can still be afraid going up into the tornado. In fact, feel into the fear of it, the confusion, the loss, whatever shows up for you – just allow it to be – that is embracing it. What we resist persists. Resistance is holding on to the cellar door, do so and it will rip you limb from limb (figuratively of course). The more you try to hold on to debris that is being hurled away – the more challenging this part will be for you.

Please take comfort in knowing that even though it may be an uncomfortable experience, the tornado of chaos is the Universe HELPING you. This reminder will help you to more easily trust that it will be OK.

Remember that every time you feel chaos or upset in your life that every breakdown before your breakthrough is simply another tornado... sending you off to Oz again to get your new ruby slippers.

'Click your heels' here - prepare to embrace the tornado...

Take a moment right now to embrace your tornado – to allow the exploration of the swirly, energy around you that you've just called into your life. Because awareness of your debris will help you to release it and/or allow it to transform.

Ponder the following questions and write down the answers that come to you. As with the remaining heel clickin' steps in this book, I'm going to ask you to be present for Toto (your intuition) to point out the symbols and signs meant to help you understand how to turn these little lead pieces of your life into gold.

embrace the tornado...

First connect to Glinda and be present for her guidance. Now, grab your journal and examine your tornado.

Where in your life are your expectations no longer meeting your expectancy? In that space is where you will find the storm. Where have you called in change... invited a new experience with your strong desire and focus on something BETTER, more joyful, happier?

What is being thrown about your energy field? In what relationships or situations are you experiencing discomfort? Are you embracing or resisting your discomfort with all your might?

What experiences, beliefs or suggestions from Kansas are MOST influencing you to hold on to the cellar doors?

Look at the debris that is falling away in your tornado and ask how it is best serving you; because it is. You may not recognize it yet. Recall, the Ruby Slipper Principles are meant to have you turned a bit around and seeing things from a new perspective!

ruby slipper principle 4: call on glinda

Call on Glinda

Because good witches stick together and help one another navigate the yellow brick road of life. At this point in your journey you have great tension to move forward despite your fears, to find your yellow brick road, to get on the journey to finally click your heels. It's time to establish lines of communication with your Higher Self.

Need some advice? Time to call on Glinda!

At this point in the heroic journey we have determined quite a few things. Most importantly, where we are *is not* where we desire to be. Just as with Dorothy who no longer wants to be in Kansas, we no longer want to be let's say in our current job, tied to something related to Corporate America, or working for the great profit of another rather than ourselves and we'd much rather be pursuing our passions - being not just successful but also fulfilled. We no longer want to silence our voices but share and shine our light. We want to contribute to a greater good. Just as Dorothy would much rather be pursuing her passions and her imagination, as she does when she sets out to save Toto.

In fact, you probably already had somewhat of an upsetting experience that has landed you with a perspective that is changed forever much like when Dorothy found herself swept up by the tornado and then landed herself in Oz. And when you begin to face those obstacles you feel a little out of sorts not quite yourself not quite sure where you're headed.

At this point, you're probably wondering if you have what it takes to continue. I believe you do and if you do, you've probably heard from others in your life, that you are really talented or inspirational; your passion is valuable and that what you would like to do... really like to do... the point B to which you strive, is something that would be so welcomed and appreciated by so many.

You are just like Dorothy; at the point when the Munchkins celebrate her landing on the Wicked Witch and she's not yet realized what she's done nor, her power, but they certainly realize her value and her service was already much needed and desired by them.

You're probably at the point in your journey where you have great tension to finally move forward, to find your yellow brick road, to get on the adventure to finally click your heels; even if it feels uncomfortable and uncertain. What Dorothy had at this point in the story is the beautiful light, support, encouragement and guidance from her very own Glinda.

Where is your Glinda?

Glinda showed up for Dorothy like a fairy godmother or spirit guide, seemingly out of nowhere. But Glinda is always present for each of us, Glinda is our higher self (*where Toto is our imagination/intuition our channel of communication*). Recall that she represents our divine feminine; our power as co-creators of our current experience.

When Dorothy manifests a conversation with her higher self a.k.a. Glinda, she can co-create the experience of the yellow brick road all the way through to clicking her heels and returning to Kansas.

Glinda is always available to you; you simply have to know how to call upon her to help you to co-create and to call on Toto to open up Divine conversations to light your path ahead.

♔ *Note*: Calling upon our higher self is different than our intuition. Toto and Glinda both guide, but Toto is an aspect of ourselves, our subconscious knowledge and Glinda is the higher self who feeds that intuition.

There are many ways to access your higher self and exercises you can do to strengthen your connection with your Glinda. In the interest of keeping it very simple and effective for you I would recommend the following as the three things you can do to most quickly make your connection:

1. Create a simple connection ritual where you set aside a few moments to get present, take a few deep breaths and set the intention to connect with your Higher Self – just have a good old fashion chat! BE patient. The messages may not stream in instantaneously at first.

   ♔ *To connect to Glinda - take 3 deep cleansing breaths and call her to the top of your head, just above your crown chakra, all you have to do is ask, the intelligence of your body will respond. Now ask for her guidance and feel into, watch, listen for the messages to arrive – trust your imagination but do not direct it.*

2. Pick up some sort of divination tool be it Tarot, oracle cards, pendulum, journaling/automatic writing, tea

leaves, bibliomancy or any other form that interests you.

> 👑 *Anyone can read tarot. Yes - even you! All you need is a deck and desire, well, and just an ounce of patience to let the messages reveal themselves to you through art. If you'd like to peek behind the deck and connect to your higher self, I'd love to invite you to check out my Intro to Tarot course available online: intrototarot.com*

3. Get your imagination flowing, the inspiration/fire spark, and use that channel and your partnership with your higher self to then begin creating your destiny. Doodle, scrapbook, write short stories, knit, paint, color... ahh the creative possibilities are so infinite.

Regardless of the method you choose, get into a space where you can open and conduct Divine conversations. You have to connect with your higher self to strengthen the channel that you have to help guide you. When you have need for guidance in any area of your life, get clear on your question, then, be present and notice the messages you receive using any of the methods listed above.

How about in 3D though? What can I do in my physical reality?

Surely it is not just me who recognizes how very difficult it is for us to see ourselves as a neutral third party would see us, to serve as witness to our Self. The fact is, many times we simply do not know what we do not know; we cannot see what we are not yet able to see and therefore it's in our best interest to call on somebody outside of ourselves who can help us to light the way.

When concepts become too 'woo woo'; or too connected to the ethereal, I like to say its time to anchor that in 3D (thank you to my friend Janie for that phrase). So, when we bring it back here to Earth how can we connect with our Glinda?

Here on Earth our connection to Glinda can be a coach, mentor, inspiration partner, even a divination tool (*if you feel you can read for yourself objectively*) that you use to open Divine Communications, even an influential book that you refer to repeatedly that gives you guidance, inspiration, a sense of empowerment and direction.

The thing about calling on the 3D version of Glinda is that any good source of third-party guidance is someone that cannot and will not take the journey for you but will share the pieces of the puzzle that take you to the next steps, they light the way just far enough ahead of you that you can see where you're going. They help to create the first steps on the bridge from point A to point B so that you don't feel as though you must leap without wings, a net, or a sense of complete and total free fall.

Good Glindas are easily accessible these days! You can find wonderful guides in facebook groups, through social media such as Instagram or even via word of mouth! One of the BEST ways to find a coach or guide is through referral.

If you're serious about living life more fulfilled and going after your dreams, then I highly recommend you consider calling on Glinda right now! Can you imagine how different Dorothy's adventure might have gone if Glinda had not pointed out the yellow brick road... if she'd not given Dorothy the assurance that she would bestow upon her magic and guidance to help her through the forest?

How to build self-confidence

Remember, familiarity breeds *confidence.* Confidence leads to action. Action leads to alleviating fears AND achieving dreams!

Often when I work with my students on connecting more deeply to their higher self and to their channels of intuition, I hear that they lack confidence, that they don't trust the information that is coming through to them. And I know this all too well myself. It took me years to feel confident enough to share my voice, to shine my light, and to feel worthy of teaching others; to feel that I really had a divine connection, an intuitive channel.

I learned this concept from Noah St. John's book, *"The Secret Code of Success"*; there are three steps to building confidence;

1. first, you experience someone who believes in you more than you believe in yourself;

2. second, you believe in another more than you believe in yourself and encourage and guide them to success;

3. third, with each successful mentoring experience that you have, you then begin to realize your own value and finally your confidence.

Dorothy builds her confidence along her journey to Oz. Recall that, like many of us, Dorothy did not get the belief and encouragement from her role models in Kansas. So, Dorothy starts at the second step (and you can too if your childhood was similar to hers), in Munchkinland; the Munchkins believe in Dorothy far more than she believes in herself. The tornado has landed her house on the Wicked Witch and suddenly she has had her first success without even realizing it. So, the Munchkins believe in her.

As she sets out on the yellow brick road, she does not quite have the confidence she needs to click her heels. But, along the way she meets the Lion, Tin man and Scarecrow and she believes in them more than they believe in themselves; she guides them to achieve their desires.

Through helping her friends find success, Dorothy too feels successful and as we all know, at the end of the story she can harness the power of ruby slippers which she gained through the clarity of knowing herself, the passion to help others and the self-confidence to act even when she was in the face of fear.

Dorothy's story is a mirror for many of us in many ways. Most especially that she doesn't leap into her adventure with all three of these characteristics solidified! In fact, if you recall the story in Kansas, Aunty Em and Uncle Henry don't believe that Dorothy can be do and have anything that she desires.

The same is true for so many of us in our lives. Often our first role models, parents, teachers, spiritual leaders and even in some cases older siblings, have their own set of fears, and expectations for us and seek to keep us safe. Perhaps it sounded something like this for you *"Your art is wonderful but, what is going to pay the bills? OR They don't call them 'starving artists' for nothing!"* So, we don't have that very crucial first step in building our own confidence; the experience of having another believe in us more than we believe in ourselves.

We then take that learned belief into adulthood, instead of our childhood guides telling us we can't do something or that our dreams are silly, to keep us 'safe'... we allow the Witch's flying monkeys (*our own doubts and fears*) to do that for us. Here is how that might show up; we have a desire to go after a dream, say to be a healer or an artist, an author or a spiritual guide and though our interest in it may be strong we tell ourselves that keeping it at the hobby stage is 'enough' for us. This passion is just something 'I'll do for myself' because I enjoy it. CERTAINLY NOT something I will ever do in exchange for money... gah! Bring on the onslaught of flying monkeys... just take me away right now... take the shoes... I'm not worthy. And stuck we are in Kansas at point A again. Boo.

Yet, it's point B we truly desire – over the rainbow for us – that's why you're reading this book right now! Therefore, it is crucial for you to go on the adventure of gaining clarity, releasing your wonderful passions, remembering your confidence and harnessing the power of your ruby slippers. It is time NOW to take the adventure to your dreams. Even if just 1 teeny step at a time, to defeat those flying monkeys and start living MORE fulfilled!

You CAN do this!

As you do, call on Glinda, connect to the source, the one who believes in you unconditionally and joyfully remembers your worth, desires and ability to shine – your Higher Self. The more you hone that connection, the more she can help you to have conversations with the Wicked Witch of the West (your Ego). A nice source of negotiation/mediation.

You may be thinking at this point... "How will I know if I'm connected to Glinda – my Higher Self?" You will know it is your Higher Self when the messages that come to you are encouraging and full of faith in you. If the messages are critical then you *must* suspect the Wicked Witch (more on her in Principle Number 11).

Remember that Glinda is the Good Witch of the NORTH, the direction of the guiding light. Your higher self is always your North Star, your guiding light.

Next, reach out to others for guidance, inspiration and support. A great first step to moving toward your dreams is to allow another to BELIEVE in you; to have faith in your dreams and your skills, ability and worth. Accept their faith in you as verification and validation that you ARE meant for MORE than Kansas.

Fair warning – if you find that you've reached out to the cellar seekers of Kansas, detach yourself graciously! You don't need their limited thinking and boundaries. ONLY accept that you have found a Glinda when what you hear are words of encouragement and support. Fear based responses to your dreams are not going to build your confidence.

Then, consciously embark upon your own heroic journey, and find ways to extend your guidance and belief in others. Just as Glinda does for Dorothy. *It is through helping others that you begin to see your true value and you build your inner strength and confidence.*

You KNOW you can help others, right? How many times have you helped another to do something that you don't necessarily feel you can do for yourself. Encouraged them to share their gifts perhaps. Had complete faith in them and their idea and encouraged them to pursue it no matter what the result? And, when they succeeded, how did you feel? I'll bet elated! Thinking or even saying *"YES! I KNEW you could do it!"* Just as the Scarecrow, Tin man, and Lion helped Dorothy.

By the way... you do NOT have to be an EXPERT in everything to help another... just be in a space of service from whatever point you are currently at.

Self-confidence is a key to your manifestation.

There are three pillars of manifestation: thought, desire, and finally action. You can desire it and think about it but that is simply not enough to manifest it in your world, you must take the action to bring it into your reality. That action, as we see with the Lion throughout the story, comes from courage and our courage comes from our confidence.

When you recognize that you are a lighthouse as Glinda is; a beacon of light for others, a mentor to illuminate the way by shining authentically and doing what I like to call passion-it-forward, the greater your light will be, and the more others will be drawn to it.

Rest assured that every time you dim your light to meet another's darkness the universe becomes confused about whether or not you are a beacon (plus it's really hard to find you in a storm and that tornado well... it's swirly so... best to be shining your light so the Universe can find you). Be clear about your passions (and by that, I mean what lights you up!), what you want to experience and feel; focus intently on that, and in being of service to others to help them reach the shore and they will joyfully show you how valuable you truly are.

You do NOT have to KNOW 'how' you, or others will reach their destination. You just must have faith in them and trust that the actions taken with the intention to live fulfilled are enough to open their yellow brick road! Glinda didn't know HOW Dorothy would progress on her path, nor which direction she would take at forks in the road... she didn't need to know that and neither did Dorothy. But Glinda had confidence in Dorothy and Dorothy had confidence that Glinda was pointing her in the right direction and thus, she began her journey.

Honor Your Bubble

Remember how Glinda appears and disappears inside of a gorgeous pink crystal ball like bubble? She shows up that way as a reminder to you to honor your 'bubble', the boundaries that you set to keep your energy elevated and protected. As a light for others, you will likely give freely of the tools, knowledge and wisdom you have gained from your journey. However, when you give too much of yourself you drain your energetic value. And we are after all, about building your confidence in your value by calling on Glinda.

Just as Glinda did for Dorothy, you can guide others, help them, encourage them, but you never do it for them or take on their battles on their behalf (empaths I'm speaking directly to you). Glinda knew those ruby slippers would only bring success for Dorothy if Dorothy used her own power. When we empower others to elevate their vibration, we elevate the vibrations of the Earth for everyone.

Now click your heels here to call on Glinda ...

Call on Glinda NOW – Build Your Confidence

First, ask your Higher Self to connect with you now. Simply take 3 deep cleansing breaths to become present and set the intention to connect.

Now ask, why do you believe in me? Allow the message to be revealed to you in whatever form comes naturally (sight, sound, vision, knowing...etc.).

Next, go 3D, ask your mentor, guide, inspiration partner or dear friend... why do you believe in me? You'll LOVE their answers I promise!

Finally, go out there and support someone else in achieving their dream! Send a shout out to a friend of encouragement. Offer up a little bit of your knowledge or skill to shine a light for someone. You are going to feel so amazing when you are acting in service.

And guess what?... That's inspired action right there that opens the possibilities for the Universe to create phenomenal coincidences and synchronicities for you to achieve your dream! WHOOT!

ruby slipper principle 5:
break free from munchkinland

Break Free from Munchkinland

The hypnotic rhythm of gumdrops and lollipops are not soul nourishing. I'll bet you have been a Munchkin and admired the bravery, courage and success of another; longing to be 'in their shoes'. And, you have just left the cellar seekers behind and earned your ruby slippers... so, here's your chance to break free and claim your own shoes.

The tornado has landed!

So here we are; house dropped right on top of a Witch in the middle of this 'new' and quite unfamiliar experience. At this point in the journey you may be feeling quite discombobulated and it will feel very tempting to return to those illusions of safety. In fact, at this point in the story, Dorothy longs to go back 'home' to Kansas.

Most often we avoid the tornado in the first place or resist it so that we can resist the uncomfortable feeling that accompanies being in a new experience. The allure of the cellar seekers is strong and we long for that feeling of 'normalcy' and safety. Settling for 'as good as it gets' is much easier than going through the dark forest to get to your dream life!

What are you to make of those Munchkins?

You have just agreed to get out of Kansas and leave the cellar seekers behind, yet here you are in Munchkinland and the folks here seem very nice... after all you have been greeted as a hero, were rewarded for your heroic efforts with song and dance and yet... something is just not quite right. Their song and rhythm are oddly familiar to you, but you can't quite put your finger on it... is this a good rhythm or is something off here. Their song and dance are the *"hypnotic rhythm"*.

The term *"hypnotic rhythm"* is something I learned from the book *"Outwitting the Devil"* by Napoleon Hill. He uses the term to describe the dull hum of the habits and limiting beliefs that become 2nd nature to us and keep us from realizing our true dream... freedom. It is what we feel as the mass consciousness.

"Any thought or physical movement which is repeated over and over through the principle of habit finally reaches the proportion of rhythm. Then the habit cannot be broken because nature takes it over and makes it permanent."

-Napoleon Hill, Outwitting the Devil

One of our most common habits is to relinquish our personal power. We freely give it away to others, especially as it relates to our spiritual beliefs. Surely, we are conditioned when we are very young to listen to the guidance of our role models, our mothers, fathers, teachers, spiritual guides. But often they have already succumbed to the hypnotic rhythm of those who shaped them, and their beliefs and it is a cycle which continues through generations.

In Oz, the Munchkins represent the mass consciousness, the hypnotic rhythm, the illusion that we are not free to be, do and have all that we desire out of life. They live in a world of gumdrops and lollipops... afraid to face their fears but pretending to be happy with the status quo.

They live, as many of us do, in fear of taking that leap OUT of convention to be the heroic one. Recall how they praise Dorothy for saving them from the Wicked Witch of the East. Yet, could they not have done the same? The Munchkins will not walk the yellow brick road on their journey to self-awareness but, will happily rely on another outside them to deal with the flying monkeys; kill the Wicked Witch for them and free them from their own hypnotic rhythm and allow them to have their own Emerald City (*success/wealth*).

Alas, you and I know relying on another to achieve for you, does not work - no one can free you from your fears except you - no one can succeed for you nor can another be responsible for your happiness. Just as Glinda could NOT tell Dorothy the secret to her ruby slippers, nor take the journey along the yellow brick road for her.

The fear of separation draws you back in.

So here you are in Munchkinland, you've decided that the cellar seekers of Kansas are not for you, you've chosen to embrace the tornado no matter how uncomfortable and despite the lovely greeting of well-meaning folks, you're still feeling unsure and unsteady in your journey.

You will likely experience enormous self-doubt in Munchkinland, as you know you don't want the old (and it didn't work for you) but you're also so uncertain about the new land that faces you up ahead.

Keep in mind that if you've made it this far on the journey it is because you have had such distaste for the status quo of your life in Kansas that you literally summoned up Source to help you manifest your desires and harness your true power. Think about that for a moment... if you are here it is because YOU manifested the tornado... YOU put the energetic forces in place to sweep you up and create the synchronicity necessary to achieve your dreams! WOW – you're good! No wonder the Munchkins are celebrating your arrival.

Here's the thing; the hypnotic rhythm is HYPNOTIC!

It will capture you and make you feel welcome and warm and safe. This is where you will hear thoughts in your head that align with the common beliefs;

- *"don't go for your dreams until you have enough money, get a new job instead"*,
- *"you can't go for that dream, you don't have the right education"*,
- *"but you're a spiritual advisor, it wouldn't be right to ask for money for your gift"*,

- *"pursuing your passion like this is so irresponsible and selfish, you have to take care of your family"*,
- and the list goes on and on.

The notes start to play one by one in your head and the lollipops and gumdrops start to look like a nourishing meal. But where are the Munchkins? Still in Munchkinland; relying on you to kill the next witch for them. The Munchkins will not take responsibility for their own freedom, but you will, won't you?

I know that the gumdrops and lollipops are tempting, the bright lights and darling little homes feel safe to you. But this is the hypnotic rhythm playing – you are in search of your own *harmonic rhythm*. Yes, there will be some loud crashes from the symbols and some piercing high notes from the flutes but, when you feel the beat of your own drum you will recognize that rhythm as your own harmony – that is the one you want to dance to!

There is no doubt that you have been a Munchkin and admired the bravery, courage and success of another; longing to be 'in their shoes' (ahhh yes, the shoes, the powerful, powerful shoes). However, at this point in the journey you have already begun your transformation from caterpillar to butterfly. The cocoon you find yourself in may feel quite comforting, warm and safe, but you will soon realize that it is just a temporary home. The caterpillars will still call to you, reminding you of the good ol' times, but you, *my pretty*, are on your way to wonderful things. You are earning your wings and filling your shoes with the divine spark that is yours by birthright.

Now follow the yellow brick road...

Following your yellow brick road is all about pursuing YOUR dreams of living life more fulfilled. When you complete this next step, I want you to do it in the context of what 'hypnotic rhythm' keeps you from voraciously pursuing the things that you most enjoy, the things you do that you are really passionate about, hobbies, activities, practices, etc.

For example, I have many spiritual practitioners in my tribe who are practicing their dreams in a really small way or behind the curtain, so they are not fully seen... be it reiki, herbology, talisman creation, divination, astrology, mediumship, reflexology, coaching, sound therapy, or shamanic healing... they have brilliant gifts and yet have found themselves dancing to the tune of the hypnotic rhythm. The Munchkins sing the song of their people, *"spiritual is too 'woo woo', get real"*, *"there's no proof so, that's fake"*, *"spiritual gifts are gifts from God, you can't charge for them"* *"divination is evil"*, *"you're in corporate, you're not spiritual"* ... *"but, since you're doing it anyway can you do it for me for free?"*.

Bet you've swayed to the hum of that rhythm as it relates to your dreams. Now, let me ask you... are you singing the song of your people or theirs? What are the songs and voices you hear repeated in the hum of your day?

Click your heels here to break free of Munchkinland...

Chewing on the lollipops and gumdrops of Munchkinland?

Take a moment right now to first connect with Glinda and recognize Toto and then grab your journal and write down a few of the most common lines that come to you.

What do the Munchkins in your life say to you? What are the societal norms that most influence you? In what ways do you feel peer pressure?

Which of the Munchkins are you listening to and why? Why do you think they are not putting on their own ruby slippers to walk the yellow brick road?

To break free of these well meaning but less than nourishing rhythms you must discern your own truth; which you can only do through knowing your Self intimately and authentically. Ok good, that's why we're here and your next step is to get out on to your yellow brick road to do exactly that!

In the meantime, review the Munchkin statements you've identified. Tune in to your heart, your center and ask if these statements are harmonic for you or hypnotic.

Do the statements come from love or fear? If fear, will you agree to release that statement/belief back to the source to become recycled and reusable energy? You can still love the Munchkins, simply cut the energetic cords to their beliefs and songs. Let's tune into a different radio frequency... ok?

Break free of Munchkinland, their dreams are not yours, their fears do not have to be yours, their gumdrops and lollipops are not soul nourishing for you. You have the ruby slippers, now go out and find your infinite power so that you can click your heels!

ruby slipper principle 6:
follow your yellow brick road

Follow Your Yellow Brick Road

It leads to profound spiritual and life alchemy. You've got the shoes, you've got the desire, and now all you need is a path. Not just any path, YOUR path to profound spiritual and life alchemy. If you desire it, you'll know and there you'll go. You can NOT take a wrong step if you are stepping in the intention of your yellow brick road.

Your path to your ruby slippers unfolds!

The Yellow Brick Road is the path to your illumination, your self-discovery, your enlightenment. It encompasses everything you need to be and do to complete your spiritual / life alchemy.

Alchemy is most commonly known as the process to turn base metals into gold and has been expanded to mean a magical process of spiritual transformation, the 'great work' which results in the universal elixir (awakening); a soul's realization and freedom.

"The search for the alchemical gold is the search for wisdom, light, perfection, and enlightenment. In historical times there was no separation between science and religion/spirituality, and thus we find (spiritual) alchemy mixed with other areas of 'science'. " ~ Dirk Gillabel, "Alchemy Intro" on House of Sun at soul-guidance.com

The Yellow Brick Road is the color of gold to represent how the heroic journey we are on reveals our own gold, the elixir of life, our awakened spirit.

It is interesting also to note here that in the book *The Wonderful Wizard of Oz*, Dorothy's shoes were silver, to represent the lead or base metal of the alchemical process – which is turned into gold as she journeys on the yellow brick road. They were turned to the beautiful ruby color only in the movie version to take advantage of the new Technicolor technology. Note how they grab your eye and intrigue you to skip along the yellow brick road, to pursue your own pair. Because of that allure, this book is called *The Ruby Slipper Principles*.

In the movie version of this story, we see that the yellow brick road begins in a spiral, the return of the Fibonacci sequence, once again reinforcing that the yellow brick road is a symbol of spiritual evolution.

Ever wanted to quantum leap into your dreams?

For Dorothy, The Yellow Brick Road is the promise of her quantum leap; it is the bridge to the Wizard. Who, in her mind, has completed a hero's journey in the past and is NOW endowed with 'special' powers to magically complete her leap for her.

"The thing about quantum leaps is that they mark an abrupt change from one state to a distinctly different one, with no in-between transitional states being possible." - Paul Brians, Common Errors in English Usage

When Dorothy asks Glinda how to get to the Emerald City Glinda says, *"You must walk. It is a long journey, through a country that is sometimes pleasant and sometimes dark and terrible. However, I will use all the magic arts I know of to keep you from harm."* - L. Frank Baum, the Wonderful Wizard of Oz (1900)

So, it would seem, a leap without doing the work or the transition phase is the thinking of the Munchkins. Spiritual alchemy is the 'great work' coined so for a reason. Glinda knew this and did not tell Dorothy the secret to her ruby slippers until AFTER she had done the 'great work' of transforming herself.

No one can do your life alchemy for you. If you want to click your heels and reveal your infinite powers, you MUST follow your own yellow brick road.

How do you walk the yellow brick road?

It starts with the awareness that you want to do the work – then you must BEGIN – take the action, take the first step, then trust your instincts (Toto) and follow the GPS coordinates provided by Source along the way.

Remember that, though the learning can only be done by you, it does not mean that you must walk your yellow brick road alone! Dorothy had Glinda to guide her and offer advice, 3 friends (the Lion, Tin man and Scarecrow) to support her and share in her journey and of course Toto to remind her to be present and alert her of dangers up ahead.

For your journey, consider incorporating all the same like-hearted players:

Who might be a good guide for you? Consider a counselor, coach, spiritual advisor, mentor; someone who understands that you are embarking on the great work of life alchemy and will need a good sounding board and inspiration partner.

I owe a great deal of my success to one of my dearest inspiration partners who was instrumental in helping me to take this book from dream to reality! Thank you, Nina! You are the Glinda of sharing my voice through my words!

Where might you find a good support group? Consider others who are like-hearted in their approach and perhaps on a spiritual journey themselves. Beware of Munchkins who want to offer you lollipops but, do NOT want to do the same type of work for themselves. You don't need someone riding your coattails; you need someone to lock arms with!

There are a vast number of fb groups available today with some wonderful folks who might fit this connection for you. Of course, you are always welcome to join us over at Ruby Slipper Rebels on fb!

Consider local in-person Meetups too. As I was finalizing this book for you, I joined a women's circle at my local metaphysical store. 13 powerfully aligned, open minded, loving and compassionate women with different dreams but like hearts. All locking arms to inspire and encourage one another, to listen and support, to give a swift jolt of accountability and a reason to go on – despite any flying monkeys or witches who sought to take our slippers from us!

I enjoyed that in-person exchange and community so much that I extended that concept now to offer Yellow Brick Road Tours – squeeee – are you ready to join us? A group of Ruby Slipper Rebels, keeping it real and helping each other to fulfill our dreams and elevate the energies of the Earth!

How will you tap into your intuition/GPS coordinates for the journey? Notice how signs arise for you; perhaps you notice angel numbers or see animals, perhaps you interpret your dreams or receive guidance during meditation, hear songs that guide you, perhaps you are fond of numerology, astrology, cartomancy, automatic writing or other forms of divination. Whatever you most notice or have an interest in making a connection with, I encourage you to keep the lines of divine communication open!

Dorothy had Toto to alert her; the Witch had a crystal ball to track Dorothy's whereabouts. I happen to be very fond of tarot and oracle cards and accessing the Akashic Records for the deeper work of energetic release.

Having conversations with Source via my cards and records has been one of the greatest gifts on my journey. It has helped me to make many critical decisions and to alert me to what is coming up in a way that no guide or friend can. In fact, much of this book was divined to me, the entire premise came in a download that I received while meditating and then it was expanded over time with the guidance of oracles and my Akashic records guides.

Follow YOUR Yellow Brick Road

At this point you might be wondering which yellow brick road belongs only to YOU. There is no ONE path to self, there is only the path that you take to self, at this time, which is ever spiraling and evolving. **Take comfort in knowing that you can NOT take a wrong step if you are stepping in the intention of your yellow brick road.**

As long as you choose yourself, you are choosing YOUR path. The only purpose in your life is to have an experience - a sometimes challenging and uncertain, sometimes joyful, abundant experience and to BE authentically YOU. The passions, desires and likes that you have inherently are there to help guide you to BE you. What you desire, desires you in return.

Set your intention for your path. How will you FEEL when you click your heels? (likely free, fulfilled and JOYFUL). Focus on that feeling and BEGIN. Visualize what experiences you might have when you feel fulfilled. Then, take inspired action toward that feeling. If you come to a crossroads pause and ask yourself which path FEELS more like you when you have clicked your heels. Watch for your GPS coordinates from Source, your signs; but know that you need only turn around IF you find yourself back in Munchkinland.

"If we walk far enough," says Dorothy, "we shall sometime come to someplace." ~L. Frank Baum, The Wonderful Wizard of Oz (1900)

Wise words from our heroine, as at some level she knew that in order to get where she wanted to go, she had to start somewhere and continue down that path, allowing the path to unfold as she went. Much like embracing the tornado, feeling the uncomfortable feeling of uncertainty – we too must just take inspired action. Take steps in the direction of your desires, no matter how small, and then just know that each next step will be revealed to you as you need it. The trick is in knowing that the step does NOT appear first – it is your faith in the step arriving and lifting your foot in full trust of landing on it that makes the step appear.

The key to unlocking the infinite power of your Ruby Slippers lays in taking the first step on your yellow brick road. NOT attempting a quantum leap, not longing for something so far beyond your reach that it makes it ok to never attain it, take just ONE step in the direction of your dreams. Then follow the yellow brick road as it unfolds.

C'mon click your heels, follow your yellow brick road...

Special reminder: I shared this with you earlier but it's worth sharing again. How do you manifest something out of nothing? WRITE IT DOWN! Yep – from the ethers, to your thoughts, to pen or pencil on paper – you will have just created something out of nothing. The creative centers of your brain are activated when you physically write it down. So, please don't skip the first step on your yellow brick road – instead skip along the yellow brick road and write down your intentions. Take a journal along with you for the adventure, because this will NOT be the only step you wish to manifest.

You're not in Kansas anymore; you've decided to break free of Munchkinland and begin the adventure down your yellow brick road...

Where is your 'somewhere over the rainbow'?

Start by getting clarity on what it is you truly desire. What is the gold over the rainbow for you?

How do you desire to feel once you've clicked your heels? WRITE it down, write down your intention. That is where you'll take your first step.

What does fulfilled feel like to you? What does happiness mean to you? How do you define freedom and how will you feel upon achieving it? How will you help others?

These statements are helping you to define where you desire to be. Which, in turn, will help you make decisions on your next steps. Your yellow brick road unfolds as you take inspired steps ONLY in the direction of your desires and elevating your consciousness. Trust me it's magical.

Now, when you call on Glinda and Toto, they will have clarity on what messages best guide you to your ruby slippers.

ruby slipper principle 7:
it's good to be king of the forest

When Intellect and Heart Meet Courage

The 3 pillars of manifestation. Elevate your company and elevate your experience. Time to lock arms with your allies to higher consciousness and manifestation! Just as Dorothy had friends to journey with her so, shall you. In fact, they are likely all around you all the time and you just do not recognize them for the gifts they bring you.

3 Pillars of Manifestation: Knowledge, Desire, and Action.

The three characters that Dorothy finds along the yellow brick road represent so much more than they appear on the surface. They represent the 3 pillars of manifestation: knowledge, desire, and action.

- The Scarecrow – our knowledge
- The Tin man – our desire
- The Lion – our courage to ACT

We need all three to manifest our desires into reality. Too often, as we see represented in the character of the Lion, we don't have the courage to act on our desires. We hide in Munchkinland or Kansas and think about our desires. Alas thinking and desiring our dreams is not enough to manifest them into our reality – we need to take action.

In fact, as I learned from Mark Passio, this is why the coronation scene in the movie Wizard of Oz is so important! It represents the critical role that courage plays in our ability to manifest. It is pointed out to us again in the poppy fields as you'll see in Principle #8 – Stay Awake in The Poppies.

"You have plenty of courage, I am sure," answered Oz. "All you need is confidence in yourself. There is no living thing that is not afraid when it faces danger. The true courage is in facing danger when you are afraid, and that kind of courage you have in plenty." - L. Frank Baum, The Wonderful Wizard of Oz (1900)

What courageous action are you taking to manifest your desires; to bring them into being?

For a LONG time, I sat confused, not understanding why the Universe hadn't delivered my dreams to my front door... after all, I asked for what I desired clearly, I had faith that it would in fact deliver, and I felt fully prepared to receive my coronation crown! Can you see why I didn't manifest my dreams? Do you now notice the flaw in my plan? I had locked arms with Scarecrow and Tin man but LION had not shown up for me, he was just chasing his tail, sitting in Munchkinland hoping that someone else would give him the courage to act.

Truly I didn't know that I wasn't doing it right. I had read so many books on manifesting and using the Law of Attraction, I really couldn't see why my dreams weren't falling in my lap. Now I KNOW that the key to manifestation is action, and not just any action, courageous action – face your Witch kind of action! Take the step on the yellow brick road without seeing the brick kind of action. YIKES!

Alas, you are not truly alone, you have friends for the journey. In fact, it's important to surround yourself with like-hearted travelers!

How will you recognize your allies?

For Dorothy it was simple, they just popped out along her journey and asked for her help. However, have you ever given pause to consider why it was that she felt a kindred spirit with each of them? She recognized them immediately. It was Hick, Huck and Zeke from the farm in Kansas! Just as our soul mates are sent to us and we feel a connection with them and don't necessarily even know why at first blush. Here, even though she was in a dream state, all the players felt familiar to her.

And just as our soul mates are encountered in real life, all these characters were sent to help her remember something about herself and her journey. In the case of the Scarecrow, Tin man and Lion, Dorothy was to remember to integrate her knowledge, desire and **courage to act** to manifest her dreams.

Your Mirrors.... You Spot it - You Got it!!

Individuals whom we encounter along the yellow brick road, IF they stand out to us or connect with us in any way (we recognize them as soul mates or allies or enemies), are mirrors for us to achieve higher consciousness. We are meant to recognize ourselves within them as they reflect back a critical piece of the puzzle for us.

In Oz, Dorothy sends the Lion to herself so that she may remember that she has the courage she needs to get Toto back, to reclaim her imagination and intuition, necessary keys to achieve her dreams.

She sends the Scarecrow to herself to help her understand that she is on the right path where she is; she has the knowledge she needs to 'outwit' the Witch but more importantly it is a message for her to take control of her mind and her imagination rather than allow the Witch (her Ego) to control it. No wonder she covets those Ruby Slippers and seeks to capture them at every turn.

The Tin man is a mirror for her to understand that what she loves and feels passion and compassion for is what she needs to act upon to find her true self which is her home.

Glinda arrives to show her how connecting with her higher self will help guide her to her true essence.

And she takes Toto along with her to be her Universal GPS system, her navigation, her intuition. Without our intuitive nudges how will we decipher which direction to go to meet coincidences along the way?

Notice in your own experience as you are traveling your own yellow brick road who you become aligned with. Have you ever complimented another on their bravery, or passion, or skill? If so, recognize yourself in that mirror.

While I was writing this chapter for you, I was on a call with a wonderful colleague and I was gushing about what a phenomenal tarot reader and intuitive guide he is for others. And in that moment remembered, he is here because I am supposed to SEE that *I* am a brilliant intuitive guide, he is simply a reflection of me. I had been questioning my gifts and my purpose (like I'll bet you have a time or two in your life) and hearing the words come out of my mouth as I was describing this chapter and what Jay was to me, helped me to recognize my own mirror! Thank you, Jay you are my Tin man, my Scarecrow and my beloved Lion!

I like to call this mirroring "*if you spot it you got it*"

- If you see the Lion in another, know you are worthy
- If you see the Scarecrow know that you are the one in control of your mind
- If you see the Tin man know that you are very compassionate and passionate and can open your heart to allow your desires to manifest in your reality

Notice the next time you compliment another and when you do, recognize that you are looking at yourself reflected in them.

Our mirrors are not here to reflect only our wonderful qualities, though I think it's very important to watch for that to help boost our confidence and validate our true beauty and essence. As we see with the Wicked Witch of the West, they also arise in our experience to teach about what we are no longer or what we would like to release from our experience.

You can look into the mirror of another and also see what you were or no longer want to be, a blessing because when you are aware of it you can dissolve it. And you'll know it's dissolved when it no longer has such a profound effect on you.

For Dorothy, the Witch is a mirror for her, showing her simply what her ego is all about, it's just an illusion of a part of 'self' who wants to survive by controlling the soul. In this case, the Witch wants to take the ruby slippers, the very essence of Dorothy's being, her infinite power to achieve freedom. The Witch is a mirror of her own doubts, fears and the beliefs which are deeply seated within her which seek to keep her small in Munchkinland or Kansas. If the Witch is NOT worthy of the slippers, it is because Dorothy questions her own worthiness to wear the ruby slippers.

The Wizard too is a mirror for her, think about it – how many times have you been 'triggered' by another, let's say someone who brags about their successes in life, but you get those hairs standing up on the back of your neck and think, that can't be true or they're NOT truly happy. This has happened too often to me when I see marketing online that feels very false to me, as if it will NOT deliver on its promises.

The trigger though is intentional; so that we 'peek behind our own curtain' and see what it is within that false feeling that is triggering us. THAT too is a mirror for us to self-reflect and ask WHY am I triggered, what is it within that which feels either true for me or brings up some anger/fear for me?

In this case, the Wizard is a reflection of what I don't want to be. I do not want to be seen as a false prophet, as someone who can NOT deliver on the transformational information as I promised in the beginning of this book. Oh dear, you've just peeked behind my curtain now.

Are you beginning to see the usefulness of the mirrors in our lives? How our reactions to people are messages for us?

Embrace the wonderful beings you meet on the yellow brick road. Look into your mirrors and see your true beauty and if you peer in and do not see 'the fairest of them all' then know that within that lies a piece of the puzzle for you.

Click your heels here down your yellow brick road...

Mirror, Mirror, on the wall, who wants to help me have it ALL?!

Reflect and direct your life toward fulfillment. Identify your divine cast of characters, collaborators and friends for this journey to Oz. For each of the archetypes, consider the people closest to you, and answer what it is you see/feel?

Scarecrow: Who do you admire for their intellect/knowledge?

Tin man: Who do you admire for their passion/desire/drive?

Lion: Who do you most admire for their courage and self-confidence?

Glinda: Who do you most admire for their self-worth?

Toto: Who do you most admire for their trust in themselves?

Wizard: Who 'triggers' you with their manipulation or false promises?

Witch: Who 'triggers' you by 'coveting' your life or an aspect of your life?

Flying Monkey: Who 'triggers' you by sharing thoughts or facts that you doubt?

Munchkin: Who 'triggers' you with expressing peer pressure?

How are each of these characters/people a reflection of you?

Why do they want to join you on your yellow brick road? What is it that they seek/desire?

For those who have most recently triggered you... how are they asking you to peek behind your own curtain?

ruby slipper principle 8:
defeat your flying monkeys

Defeat your Flying Monkeys

Because fears and limiting beliefs serve only to send you back into Munchkinland. Along the way to your desires, you will encounter societal norms, fervent religions, and media messages, developed to control you through fear. The Witch truly hopes that her advertising is working on you and soon enough you'll turn your slippers over to her.

Enter the flying monkeys!

As you walk your yellow brick road of spiritual enlightenment and illumination, there are bound to be challenges. Enter those pesky flying monkeys!

They present themselves when you don't recognize your divine worth and you allow yourself to be drained of your source of spiritual gifts. They can be seen and are most influential when the traditions and beliefs you have come to accept from your childhood in Kansas are being challenged and tested.

The yellow brick road is after all your search for self. And who are you, truly? Are you allowing yourself to be defined by the roles you've been expected to fulfill or are you ready to harness the infinite power of the ruby slippers you have just earned when you landed in Oz and agreed to take this heroic journey?

What are these flying monkeys really?

Remember that the Witch represents your Ego and the flying monkeys are the slaves to her domain, nothing more than the Ego launching doubtful thoughts your way, meant to scare you and try to keep you in the hypnotic rhythm. They seek to send you back to Munchkinland, to take your power (your shoes) away from you and feed you gum drops and lollipops instead.

You'll find that they pop up to plant seeds of self-doubt; to whisper nasty little statements to you which will have you questioning yourself and your path.

Wouldn't it just be easier to go back to Munchkinland and have Glinda watch over you there?

These monkeys are much like societal norms, fervent religions and, media messages, developed to control us through fear. The Witch wants desperately for her programming to work on you so that soon enough you turn your slippers over to her.

But please do stop for a moment to discern... are the doubts, the statements you hear in your head, actually TRUE? Would another person say it was true for you; about you? If not, it's simply a pesky monkey.

Why are we so bound by these creatures?

We truly think that we don't have any control or choice in the matter, we didn't ask for them, the Witch has sent them, and therefore we must avoid them or be captured. But we do have a choice when they arrive; we can choose to face them, feel them and dissolve them, or to believe them and succumb to them. It's just that both of those choices feel painful to us so, we duck our heads and hope to avoid them all together.

This is how the Witch controls us, it's so simple, she sends out just a few strong but doubtful thoughts to keep us guessing. The doubts we are thinking then turn into a feeling that no matter what we do, we get the same results;

so, we keep 'trying' to avoid them and hide from them hoping that we will get rid of them; they keep us in a perpetual state of fear. Which serves to further disillusion us; we fear failure, success or separation so much that we simply paralyze ourselves. We feel we can't take another step forward or experience another flying monkey.

How can you continue down your yellow brick road and swat those flying monkeys out of the sky?

Remember that our thoughts and our feelings are not enough to manifest our desires; we must also take inspired action. In this case, you must harness your inner Lion and with the confidence of a KING, harness the true essence of your courage, KNOW that you are worthy and simply demand your birthright.

If you find yourself in the Dark Forest, know that you have embarked on a great adventure. With each step forward your confidence grows, the false whispers, the doubts, the fears, start to crumble away and wash right through you – *that is how you defeat the flying monkeys – just keep acting forward!*

For example, you might be thinking about sharing a new skill with the world in a professional sense; let's just take a spiritual practice such as tarot reading as an example because I happen to be surrounded by lovely readers and healers who find themselves plagued by the monkeys. Now, you go to put a price on your services and what happens? For me, in the beginning, MONKEY mind flooded in! *"You're not worthy of charging", "You don't even know what you're doing", "You're not an expert", "They'll know you're a fraud"* ... oh gosh that's a long dark forest to go through for sure.

So, I asked my trusted friend, *are these statements true?* Because THIS is what I'm hearing in my head and I'm afraid to go forward and offer my services. Of course, my friend AND other clients vehemently opposed ALL the statements. They all had complete faith in me and thought I was helpful, worthy and quite 'gifted' at reading.

Hmmm... so, those monkeys are just 'fake news' from the Witch? Yep!

But it doesn't end there... what happened next? Did the fear just dissipate as I sat there? NO. Did the thoughts go away because someone else said I was being silly? NO. How then did I end up offering professional readings? I felt the fear and offered my services anyway! Yep – I went uncomfortably into that 1st reading. I doubted, I sweat, I struggled, I even stammered. I questioned if I was truly helpful afterwards and then, accepted payment and did it again and again. And over time, would you know... the flying monkeys started to dissipate. They had no power over me. I had summoned the courage to act because familiarity brought confidence!

Toto Alerts You!

When you feed the monkeys and dwell on the doubts they deliver, they will grow in number and strength and you will be calling upon yourself an army of monkeys even more difficult to overcome.

Instead, give thanks for your infinite power, focus on your ruby slippers pick 'em up and just put one foot in front of the other, moving forward toward your dreams of fulfillment and joy. Remember that those monkeys are powerless to do more than simply transport you closer to the entrapment of your Ego voice.

"Fake News"

The Witch's advertising and programming is powerful, and it can be seen almost everywhere in your life, at work, home, on television, on the internet and through nearly every activity you encounter. Rather than simply accept the 'fake news' you are receiving, challenge those monkeys! Swat them down and continue on your way...

Now go defeat some of those flying monkeys!

As we have in the other chapters, use this time to call on Glinda and Toto. Take your deep breaths, align with your intentions and grab your journal. Write down the answers you find to the following questions:

- Where are the flying monkeys showing up in your life? Where do you doubt your worth, your ability?

- When do they show up for you?

- How do they show up?

- If you were to peek behind their curtain what truth would be revealed? Ask yourself, would [insert your dearest friend's name here] say this is true about me or my services?

- Now ask yourself, would you be willing to move forward anyway, knowing that it may be uncomfortable, if you were assured it would result in the manifestation of your dreams fulfilled? If not, why not?

How to Release the Flying Monkey Energy – Shift your energy NOW!

BONUS ADVENTURE

How to release flying monkey energy

Let's venture into the dark forest together, knowing the monkeys await us and practice swatting a few of them down!

C'mon, let's play with our powers and become familiar with how it might feel to be so courageous and powerful. Because familiarity leads to confidence and confidence leads to action and actions lead to manifestations of our dreams... cool right?

Recognizing the doubts is the first step to releasing the flying monkeys and yet, it is here where we tend to hide in life. Even in the story, don't you want for all the characters to hide behind a tree or in the dark forest unseen when you know the monkeys are approaching?

Yet, the monkeys are nothing more than limiting beliefs that paralyze us – that no one else would agree to or say is true about us.

Here is a great process to help shift your energy and swat those flying monkeys down.

Grab your journal and write down the following questions and their answers.

- What is the flying monkey? (What am I thinking? What is the doubt I am currently experiencing?)
- How does that make me feel?
- Therefore, what action am I taking on it (based upon my feelings)?
- And what do I have as a result?

Now go through the questions again but this time *in the opposite voice* to release that flying monkey energy.

- What would be the opposite of that doubt/the 'truth'?
- How would I feel if the opposite were true?
- What action would I take if the opposite were true?
- And what would I have as a result of that action?

This is a way of moving through the dark forest and becoming familiar with the monkey because with familiarity comes confidence!

Example: Here's an example of my own flying monkey energy release (*clearly it helped because you are now reading this book!*)

Flying monkey shows up....

I think: the information in my book is horrible, nobody is going to want it, nobody is interested in it, it doesn't make sense, I have no credentials to write it, I'm not a trained author; I have no right to be writing this book.

Therefore, I feel: unworthy of releasing it, nervous and anxious, scared about putting it out in the world.

So, the action I'm taking is: I write a little bit and fall asleep in the poppies for a long time, I write a little more and fall asleep in the poppies for a long, long time (6+ years in the making so far).

And what I have as a result is: an ever-growing outline, thousands of words on a page and... nothing more than a stuck desire and un-manifested dream.

BUT, what of those flying monkeys... if the opposite were true?

If I thought: This is a book that is well done, it's transformational, people cannot wait to read and receive it.

Then how would I feel? I'd feel very welcomed and embraced and eager and excited. Just typing this I can already feel it changing in my stomach as if the butterflies are ready to be released in anticipation of a WONDERFUL flight.

So, the action I would take is: I'd be finishing and publishing this book NOW, right now. I'd be so excited to see what information is unfolding in my process.

And then what would I have? A book to share with the world! Ha and another item to check off of my 'Ta Da' list!

Were you able to feel the shift in the energy as I did when I typed through that exercise? Try it; I think you'll find the process uplifting and a great way to release yourself from the clutches of those pesky monkeys.

ruby slipper principle 9:
stay awake in the poppies

Stay Awake in the Poppies

Avoidance will not get you to the Emerald City. You're almost there! The stronger the pull to sleep, the closer you are. Now is the time to tap into Glinda (your divine feminine creative power) and ask for help. Brrrr, I feel the snow falling.

Are You Asleep in the Poppies?

As Dorothy and her friends approach the end of the yellow brick road they see the Emerald City in the foreground. They are so close now to the Wizard that they can taste it! In their excitement they rush forward off the yellow brick road and into the field of poppies... but then, they feel very sleepy and decide to maybe just rest for a small bit.

The Witch has cast a spell on them. Just as our Ego seeks to keep us asleep to our true infinite power because that power will set us free. Often it is our Ego that whispers those sour nothings in our ear; *you're not good enough, you can't do it, you'll be embarrassed, you can't earn money this way,* etc.

Now think about how this has come true for you in your life. Ever been really close to a goal and just decided to stop and rest for a bit? I can't tell you how many times I began writing a chapter for this book and was on a great roll when... oooh, a notification on facebook... I'll just check it out quickly. And then I'd have drifted off for an hour or a day or month or more on my little nap.

Poppies, the Representation of Addiction

The poppies are a representation for our addictions (think about it for a moment, poppies = opiates/heroin) – our desire to numb out or avoid rather than face our fears and challenges head on.

A dear friend once gave me the profound gift of sharing with me that the Latin root of the word addiction is "addicio" from ad ("to, towards, at") + dicio ("say; declare") meaning to say.

"Loreen, addiction is familiar to all of us. The latin root of the word is addicio – which means voice. Whenever you felt you

158

lost your "voice" you were in the turmoil of addiction. People find traditional addiction as a way to drown out the pain of not having a voice. The thoughts and feelings they suppress and never express through their voice – either written or spoken. Addicted just means voice shut down. When people speak their truth, healing begins." ~ MarciaAnn Lubore

That was one of the most eye-opening moments of my life! Thank you MarciaAnn for that life-altering change in my perspective. I had NO IDEA that I had been in a state of addiction. Why would I think that? I had such a narrow view of what addiction might be that I couldn't have fathomed before that, that I had an addiction to my own silence. It made me aware that my pattern of falling asleep in the poppies was when an opportunity arose to share my voice (my opinion/thoughts, my truth) loudly, clearly and with strong conviction... I'd just find an excuse to remain quiet.

That is the moment that Glinda came in and threw a little snow on Dorothy to wake her up. When we have awareness like that, we can begin our healing and we can begin to take back our power and get back on track toward our dreams.

With that insight, I was personally able to release my own voice! Shortly after that realization and while speaking to MarciaAnn, the Oznalogy was born. My channels of communication were busted wide open and I 'downloaded', 'channeled', however you like to describe communication from Source, the archetypes of Oz and how they mirror our heroic journey.

Never question how powerful a little snow from Glinda can be! At that point, I was well on my way to the Emerald City.

The Lion Sleeps

Did you notice in the movie that Dorothy and the Lion fall asleep, but the Tin man and the Scarecrow do not? Why might that be? Let's go back to the 7th Principle for just one second and revisit the 3 pillars of manifestation: thought, desire and action, the poppies are yet another symbol to us that desire (the Tin man) and thought (the Scarecrow) are not enough to achieve our dreams. We need action to truly manifest our dreams.

So, what happens then? When we approach success our courage to act, our willpower, literally drifts away; we become fearful and our courage gets a bit sleepy on us. We tend to numb out as we get close to success. We often choose one of our addictions to avoid our goal, from shopping to checking in on social media or checking emails and suddenly we find ourselves drifting off again away from the manifestation of our desires; anything to keep us from taking action.

Why do we stop? Because our fears are a real thing folks! I think the young folks today would say #thestruggleisreal. But the litany of reasons we experience fear all seem to be related to our wonderful characters of Oz: we fear we're not worthy (Tinman), we fear we're not smart enough (Scarecrow), we fear we are weak (Lion), we fear we will fail (Wizard), we fear our own power (Witch) and all seem to amount to... we fear we will not be accepted or we will be abandoned (Kansas - oh that's a big one for me)!

And too often, we just don't realize how close we are to truly have our dream fulfilled... so we 'take a small break'. As a personal example, I had this book outlined for 5 years, FIVE YEARS! And I've picked it up time and time again and the moment that a chapter seems to be difficult, or a friend told me just how profoundly wonderful it was, or I was nudged by the Universe with an Oz reference begging for this thing to be released... I'd just fall asleep in the poppies. This has been one long nap in the poppies!

"It takes courage to endure the sharp pains of self-discovery, rather than choose to take the dull pain of unconsciousness that would last the rest of our lives." – Marianne Williamson

The Wakeup Call...

Back in Oz, Glinda offers a little help to Dorothy and her friends; she sprinkles snow on them, releasing the sleep spell of the poppies. Glinda, the representation of our divine feminine creative power, sends a powerful message to us at this point in the story. Her intervention is a reminder to us to tap into our divine feminine creative powers to co-create that which we desire. Often our strength and courage comes from within and can be re-ignited when we tap into our infinite power.

Fair Warning... the snow also freezes the Tin man! A powerful reminder that we can easily become jaded and disheartened when we don't see results of our creativity quickly enough. Our passion for it literally freezes and once again we find ourselves stuck in the poppies and not taking action.

The Emerald City is very close now, you're almost there! The stronger the pull to sleep, the closer you are.

Stay Awake in the Poppies!

Check in with yourself right now and see where it is you might be asleep in the poppies. Do you have a dream sitting on the shelf; an idea that floats stagnant in your thoughts; a book yet unwritten, a passion yet unexpressed?

If so, then let's put a little snow on you to wake you back up!

1. First, you've just become aware that you are asleep in the poppies – yay you, step 1 awareness!

2. Second ask yourself, which aspect of your self is sleepy? What is it that you are trying to avoid? Where has the Witch (your Ego) cast her nasty spell upon you?

Here let me guide you just a bit... which of these characters is holding you back?

Tinman: If there was NO WAY you could fail, if you had more millions than you could spend in a lifetime, if all 'ordinary obstacles' were gone (as they are in the poppy field) would you move forward with your pursuit of the Emerald City? If not, then it is your passion which is not ignited on that dream.

Your poppies: "you've no burning desire for this particular project, dream"

Scarecrow: If you had all the certifications, took all the 'right courses', had all the skills to be a master at this, would you move forward with your pursuit of the Emerald City? If not, then it is your thoughts, which are holding you back.

Your poppies: "you don't think you have what it takes to achieve"

Lion: If your audience were longing for you, singing your praises, fanatically sharing your glorious expression with others, begging to work with you and pay you handsomely for time in your court, would you move forward with your pursuit of the Emerald City? If not, then it is simply your courage to act that has you chasing your tail – afraid of your own shadow.

Your poppies: "you are afraid of your own power, afraid of success"

Toto: If all of your intuitive nudges were clear, precise and strong, if synchronicities were obvious to you and you were always in 'the right place at the right time' would you move forward in pursuit of the Emerald City? If not, then it is your imagination, the gateway to your intuition, your relationship with your intuitive gifts which are holding you back. Unlike Toto, you are not living in the present – you are living in the past or the anxiety of the future.

Your poppies: "you're not living in the present moment"

Kansas: If your parents, friends, teachers, entire community all believed in you fully, encouraged you to move forward and knew beyond a shadow of a doubt that your dream should be pursued, would you then move forward in pursuit of the Emerald City? If not, then you are stuck in a hypnotic rhythm of your own making.

Your poppies: "you don't know who you truly are; you don't know your harmonic rhythm"

You've taken steps 1 and 2 – you're aware you're asleep in the poppies and now you know which aspect(s) of Self is making you sleepy time for step 3...

3. Sprinkle a little snow on yourself! You now know what your poppies are; the snow is the antidote to the spell. Now is the time to tap into your divine feminine creativity – have a conversation with Glinda – ask for guidance to address any or all of the areas listed above which have you sleepy.

You can call on Glinda at any time, she is your higher self and when you call upon your higher self she will respond. Right in this moment, take the time to connect with your higher self.

Here's a quick snow machine for you: take 3 deep breaths, close your eyes and call your Higher self to the top of your head (the 8th chakra just a couple of inches above your crown, is where you get access to expand your consciousness and transcend above your 3D perceptions; it's where the energy of your Higher Self can help you connect – not a chakra course here but, valuable information just the same). Greet your Higher self and ask for guidance. Be willing to simply be present and aware in that moment and be patient. You may not notice the messages received immediately but, the answers will come to you, watch for ideas that arrive/signs that appear, it might be within moments, hours or even days of requesting the information but, it WILL arrive if you remain present to it.

The lesson in the poppies is the power of being present and aware. Remember that the Witch (your Ego) will always try to pull you back into the hypnotic rhythm of sleep and inaction. When you hear those sour nothings in your ear, know that is the Witch saying, *"I'll get you my little pretty... and your dog too!"*

Wake up from the poppies... click your heels here to head to the Emerald City...

What has you so sleepy?

What happens when you begin to take steps toward your dreams?

What distracts you most? In what ways do you fall asleep in the poppies?

Which character listed in this chapter most resonated with you? Which poppies did you find yourself asleep in? Was it your skills, your passion, your courage, your presence, your hypnotic rhythm... a combination (a bouquet of sleepy poppies perhaps)?

Take some time to write the answers down and then go back to the snow machine exercise and call on Glinda to ask for some SNOW to wake you up and help you to move forward.

ruby slipper principle 10:
peek behind the wizard's curtain

Peek Behind the Wizard's Curtain

The answers are not in false prophets or illusions of worthiness. You are worthy by birthright, equipped with all the necessary pillars of manifestation but, in order to reveal them you must go within and connect to your intuition.

Broomstick Challenge

The first real disappointment sets in when Dorothy reaches the Emerald City and despite overcoming those sleepy poppies she is met again with resistance. First, they are denied entry to the city, so she exerts more courage to press on and demand access to the Emerald City to see the Wizard.

Upon entering, they have to pretty themselves up in order to be worthy of meeting the Wizard. This process is symbolic of how we put on false outward appearances to show our 'value'; of how our 'material possessions' are a reflection of our inner value and yet, this too is a false illusion.

Once they finally get in front of the Wizard, Dorothy is asked to take on even more responsibility; he tells them that they must capture and offer him the Witch's broomstick BEFORE he will grant their wishes.

Where have we seen this lack of courage before? In Munchkinland! The Munchkins want for Dorothy to kill the Wicked Witch of the West, they are not willing to venture out and do it themselves. Now, the Wizard who is doing everything in his power to make them feel unworthy of his 'powers', is exhibiting the same fear and lack of courage to act on his own. Such projection!

He sends the group off to get the Witch's broomstick for him. This is an even more difficult stage as Dorothy will be asked to take her courage to the next level and face her fears HEAD ON. She will be asked to take full responsibility for all aspects of her being. This is the stage of the heroic journey that truly FIRES us up!

Note to Self: Part of knowing your Self and your inner power so intimately is accepting responsibility and accountability for all parts of yourself. As you strip away the stories you tell yourself, the hypnotic rhythms you've accepted, the flying monkeys you've succumbed to, and you face and accept your shadows (capture the Witch's broomstick) ... you reveal your true power. Awareness is a critical first step, then acceptance, then forgiveness and finally, the shift of your inner world is manifested in your outer world; not just for you, but for all of us!

You are NOT the Fairest of Them All

Remember that The Wizard is also a mirror for Dorothy. She recognizes his message/puzzle piece for her since she encountered him first in Kansas as Professor Marvel. There he used sleight of hand to take a picture of Auntie Em out of her basket when she was not looking and then used that information to feign his 'psychic' ability. He uses that to fool her into going back home – to stay in Kansas.

In Oz, the Wizard is a mirror of unworthiness. He does not feel worthy and acts as a false prophet / magician and at this point in the journey Dorothy and her friends feel unworthy as well. She is not yet ready to click her heels as she still believes that the answers to her transformation are outside of her with the Wizard.

As with any impactful heroic journey there must be challenges along the way; here the heroine learns to overcome by using her innate gifts. The Wizard serves a wonderful purpose in this story to put a huge obstacle in Dorothy's way which, she must overcome to be deemed worthy of earning his favor.

Believing fully that once this challenge is overcome the Wizard will help her and her friends; Dorothy sets out to capture the Witch's broomstick. This is it, she's mustering up the courage to take ACTION toward her dream!

Beware of False Prophets and Illusions of Worth

Upon her return to the Emerald City with the broomstick, the Wizard needs more time to stall as he knows he has no special powers and is nothing more than a fraud, he becomes more and more furious with Dorothy and her friends and insists that they come back the next day.

Often, we become angry out of fear, fear of not being worthy, being wrong, being right; when that anger arises in you, ask yourself what it is that you are afraid of and perhaps unwilling to face. The Wizard feared that his truth would be revealed, that he is not capable of magic at all.

After overcoming the obstacle of capturing the Witch's broom using all of her faculties, Dorothy is far more in tune to her intuition and this is when Toto pulls back the curtain on the Wizard to reveal that he is nothing more than a common man – just like Dorothy – an 'ordinary' person - no superhero, no prophet, no wizard, nothing more than any of us.

Just as we become more in tune with our gifts with every obstacle we overcome. Most often we have to access our intuition in order to be able to overcome our challenges... it's a muscle that we need to develop to have the inner strength to persevere.

The crew insists that the Wizard deliver on his promises of a brain, a heart, courage and a way home for Dorothy. To save face, he gives each of them a false representation of what they really want; for the Scarecrow a diploma, for the Tin man a ticking heart clock and for the Lion a medal. But, these are just illusions and symbols; they are not the truth of our worthiness or our success.

The Wizard hides behind the curtain, just as many of us hide behind our diplomas, certifications, medals, trophies and masks. But those are simply false illusions that imprison us. We are worthy by birthright, equipped with all the necessary pillars of manifestation but, in order to reveal them we must go within. We cannot rely on false prophets, quick fixes, shortcuts or people outside of ourselves to take courageous action on our behalf or bestow upon us our gifts.

And this shows up in our lives all the time doesn't it? Perhaps in the form of a life coach who insists you can't get ahead unless you have a life coach; a marketer who claims there's a surefire way to make a six-figure income and leave your day job, but you must get 'this system' or fail; a celebrity figure who says they lost 30 pounds using this pill which is so easy and you can too. Any of these Wizards ringing a bell for you?

The more alert you are, the more you tune in to Toto, the more obvious the Wizards of life become.

Where are you a Wizard hiding behind a curtain?

"Dorothy said nothing. Oz had not kept the promise he made her, but he had done his best. So, she forgave him. As he said, he was a good man, even if he was a bad Wizard." - L. Frank Baum, The Wonderful Wizard of Oz (1900)

I think there is a key lesson in the quote above, and that is: even though many of us hide behind our own curtains every day, it doesn't make us bad people it simply means we are less than accomplished at creating our realities as we desire in an authentic way.

How often have you been told to *"fake it 'til you make it!"*? And how does that feel? I have too often on my adventures to Oz pretended, like the Great and Powerful

Oz to be something more than I am; tried to make myself believe that I was simply going to force myself into success by acting successful. And do you know how vulnerable I felt? How intensely I protected my facade, to keep others from seeing that I truly didn't know what I was doing. It's a very uncomfortable place to be.

Listen to THIS Great and Powerful TRUTH from Glinda (no Wizard speak) ...

You were sold a load of hooey in Kansas if you bought into 'fake it 'til you make it'. And there is a way to come out from behind your curtain and have Dorothy and her friends adoring you...

1. Forgive yourself for being inauthentic.
2. Forgive those in Kansas who held and then imprinted their belief on you that it was the only way for you to get ahead.
3. Come out of the curtain! Be who you are, fully, truly, in all your authenticity. You're NOT a bad person, you're a bad faker.

The Wizard had many wonderful talents, he was a charismatic leader, a confident charmer and he could inspire a crowd. He was also a bit of a chameleon, did you notice in the movie how he showed up in a few roles, the doorman to the Emerald City, the horse and carriage driver and of course, the Wizard. Sometimes we simply don't know how to express and value our gifts. That doesn't mean that we have to fit into someone else's mold to succeed.

Vulnerability is a powerful tool of creative energy and the light on the path to your yellow brick road. I believe that Brené Brown stated it well...

"Vulnerability is the birthplace of love, belonging, joy, courage, empathy, and creativity. It is the source of hope, empathy, accountability, and authenticity. If we want greater clarity in our purpose or deeper and more meaningful spiritual lives, vulnerability is the path."

— Brené Brown, Daring Greatly

So indeed, coming out from behind our curtains is KEY to manifesting our desires. Darn, I was hoping to do this without being vulnerable... you? (wink)

Yes, each of us must overcome great challenges to release our fears and realize our courage. But then, we can peek behind our own curtains, come out from behind our masks and reveal our true nature.

Now, go peek behind curtains!

peek behind your own curtain

Take 3 deep cleansing breaths, connect with Glinda and Toto. Now, explore areas in your life where Wizards show up — internal and external.

What curtain are you hiding behind? Where in your life do you pretend, exaggerate, or put on false airs to impress another, to fit in with the crowd, to appear worthy to another? How does it feel to you?

Where do you seek out Wizards in your life: quick fixes, shortcuts, gurus...?

When you peek behind your own curtain into the shadows you acknowledge the fallible, yet worthy and loveable human that you are being. FORGIVE yourself for any Wizardry that has come up here. No judgment just love and compassion for self.

You may be wondering 'how' to forgive... if so, one of the best methods I've found is Ho'oponopono, a Hawaiian forgiveness and healing technique developed by Dr. Hew Len. The mantra is: "I love you, thank you, I'm sorry, please forgive me". Simply repeat the mantra over and over again while thinking of the answers to your questions above and allow the thread to lead you where it may. You may find your mind wander to have conversations with your higher self and you may also find profound release and healing. As emotions arise – allow them to express through you. I encourage you to learn more about this phenomenal practice if it so moves you.

ruby slipper principle 11: pour water on your witch

Pour Water on the Witch

Her desire is mind control, yours is freedom. The time has come to face your fears, release your limiting beliefs and free yourself. Remember there is no manifestation without inspired, courageous action.

Time to face the Witch and capture the broomstick!

You are almost home! So close you can taste it now!

So, this is it, the BIG one, the big fear! We have come to the point on our journey where, we are faced with the ultimate challenge, we must slay the dragon to take the castle and have our dream come true. In this wonderful adventure we call life... a dream that we have created for ourselves... we manufacture a way to prove our own worth of our ultimate desire. We must finally face the Witch and grab her broomstick.

Up until this point on the journey Dorothy has been able to muster through without facing her deepest fear. Don't we all hope that we'll be able to harness the power of our ruby slippers without any pain and suffering... without having to *slay the dragon*? Until this point on her journey she is holding out hope that the Wizard will save her, that he will take her back home and magically help her friends achieve their dreams as well.

Alas, there is no spiritual alchemy without facing the fire! And there is no manifestation of our dreams without the courage to act. We can think about it, really, really want it but, that's just not enough. Sorry folks but we've already seen that desire (Tin man) and thoughts (Scarecrow) cannot make it to the Emerald City without Courage (Lion) and taking physical action. We've got to muster up the courage to take inspired action.

Who is the Witch you must face?

The Witch, who represents Ego, will rear her ugly head in any situation which threatens to separate her from control.

She wants to hold Dorothy back - keeping her 'separate' from her connection to herself, her power, her voice (those beautiful ruby slippers). Just as our ego seeks to keep us from any change which seems threatening to its survival.

Why do you think she keeps going after the dog? Without imagination and intuition, we have no clear channel to the Divine, no way to co-create what we desire, no desire to get 'outside the box' and be free. She wants the imagination and intuition as well; the key to the power!

Think of a time when you ventured out of your comfort zone... did you feel any fear? If so, that was your Ego trying to keep you from venturing out.

The Color of Money

Note that in the film version of the story, the Wicked Witch is green - the color of money. Symbolic, as it is what we are taught is our source of self-value and what we are to 'love'/desire; wealth - the definition of success in society. Now think of how your relationship with money shapes and defines your self-worth, your very definition of your own success/worthiness.

Are you beginning to see how profound this story is for us? We desire freedom to be, do and have anything we desire, we want to pursue our true passion in life, our soul's

181

purpose to be fulfilled and yet we are conditioned to believe that our value, our self-worth is shown by *money*. Our Ego then works to attain and keep money at any cost. This is why so many of us have difficulty leaving even a miserable job or cutting back on our income by so much as a penny to pursue what we truly love.   If money were no object, what would you be and do? I'm going to venture a guess to say it's not currently what you are doing.

Now you know, the obstacle between where you are now: *Kansas*, and where you want to be: '*home*' is the Witch! That is not to say that all fears are equal and that we all fear the loss of money or success, there are other aspects to the Witch. But, I think it's profound to point out how she represents the 'status quo', the accepted norm of success, our 'value'. She is what keeps us from sharing our authentic voice, our true value, our desire for freedom and independence.

Our Ego would have our imagination in a basket, contained and well under control and many times, it does! Are you using your imagination... connecting with your intuition? Doing everything you can to co-create your freedom, the experience of your dreams? If not, who or what is the Witch you face? (Wait... let me give you a clue... she is within YOU.)

Pouring water on the Witch

Here's where our imagination tends to run wild, we make the battle against the Witch much, much scarier than it must be! She has powerful control over our mind. Remember that whenever we veer out to walk our yellow brick road she sends those pesky monkeys, the flying doubt monsters who whisper into our ear terrible sour nothings which would have us believing that we're not good enough, not creative enough, not strong enough, we don't know our true passion or purpose. She works every step of the way to fill us with uncertainty and the belief that we are much safer in Munchkinland.

The thing is that the Ego will always try to control the mind and with it the imagination and therefore your slippers (*recall how those flying monkeys capture the Scarecrow in the dark forest and tear out all his straw? A symbol of controlling and scattering the mind*). BUT, do remember that the Witch is easily dissolved with water. As Dorothy reaches out to save her friend the Scarecrow from certain death by fire, the water from the bucket hits the Witch and she simply melts away. The same is true for our fears, when we face them, really face them, head on, eyes open, our awareness of them and willingness to experience them and forgive ourselves for them, will dissolve them and they will no longer have a hold over us.

This is not to say that poof the fear dissolves because we are aware of it... there is the process of filling the water in the bucket; water is symbolic of our emotions. To pour water on the witch is to face the fear AND FEEL the experience. The 'water' is in the feeling, the emotions that we release.

What is your Witch?

What is it you are afraid to face? For me, it was falling asleep in the poppies for years, avoiding looking at my finances – I knew that would be my *Water on the Witch* moment. I knew that if I looked at them, REALLY opened my eyes to what was going on, it would be terribly painful. My 'value' was dwindling, with no source of replenishment.

By the time I mustered up the courage to look, it was too late, it was all gone. My deepest fear realized. We had no money; house in foreclosure, no income, no jobs, no retirement savings, NO MONEY. Let me tell you that it was terrible to look at, to realize; and it felt AWFUL, I cried, a LOT, I felt worthless and defeated for a while. BUT, when I faced it ... the FEAR dissolved. I was FREE, I no longer had a FEAR of losing all my money. And never again have I been afraid of facing my financial situation. I can now look my money straight in the eye and say it is I who control you – not the other way around. I do not fear money or lack of money any longer. My value is no longer attached to my bank account. Think about that, it's a powerfully freeing moment and experience.

I know what you're thinking... *No, facing that situation did not then bring me vast riches*, it simply dissolved the fear that was holding me back. I was able to take back control from the Witch and that is a click your heels energy boost for sure!

Here's another example, many folks fear losing their job and the fear eats away at them as the pending loss hangs over their head day after day and permeates every area of their lives. Then, the call comes, the HR person or manager arrives with 'the packet' and poof the job is gone. Does that person now fear losing their job? NO – the fear is gone. You can't fear losing that which you don't have. Oh sure, you may now feel uncomfortable and discombobulated because this is the point where the tornado has just swooped you up and dropped your house on the Witch! But, even in the confusion and the debris that you didn't want to lose just getting cast off in that tornado - remember that you just earned your ruby slippers! You are freed now for a great adventure.

Nifty tip about Witches: Where there is smoke there is fire, at least that's a thing people say. And I can tell you that when you avoid smoke and avoid the fires when they are newly sparked, they grow, exponentially and can get quickly out of control. Then, it takes oceans of water to put out those forest fires.

For example, had I faced that fear much earlier in my journey, it would have been but a small flame rather than a huge forest fire! If I would have just looked at my finances, even though it would have been painful to see them draining, I would have been able to choose a more empowered action and perhaps change the trajectory of my future. All the more reason to pour water on your witches often and early!

What happens when you face the Witch?

Just as with Dorothy, once you face the fear and allow the feelings to rush through you, you are FREE. You are free to evolve, to now see this journey from a new, more elevated perspective. This Witch is the catalyst for your soul's expansion.

This is the final stage of your spiritual alchemy – you are able to access the gold within you. And with each Witch you face and pour water upon, the next gets easier and easier. You will find that your highs are even higher and that your lows not nearly as low (or scary) because you have evolved.

Click your heels here to dissolve your Witch...

time to face the witch

Call on Glinda and Toto and ask: What is the situation that I most avoid? Why? She is the Witch you must face right now.

Asking and allowing the answer is the first step - it means becoming acutely aware of her.

Next, accept that you've been avoiding her and allowing her to hold you back.

Now, face her head on: have the difficult conversation, uncover the difficult information,

Now grab your bucket and pour! Allow yourself to feel the emotions of grief (because you are about to 'lose' something – a pattern, belief, relationship, addiction, comfortable lie, an excuse, a false sense of security, etc.). Release – cry, bawl even, the really ugly snotty kind if you must.

Now, forgive yourself! You have disempowered her and may now capture her broomstick and click your heels.

Congratulations! I am so very proud of you! That is NOT EASY. It sounds simple, but I've been there, it's no small task and can be a very draining experience (all the water, remember). But that release is what will set you FREE.

Facing the Witch takes serious COURAGE. Give yourself credit, display that broomstick with pride, you've earned it.

ruby slipper principle 12: click your heels

Click Your Heels

Harness your infinite powers to manifest your desires. This is it! You've landed in Oz. You have been awarded a pair of ruby slippers and it is your Soul's purpose to click them and your life's purpose to find your way home to a life fulfilled.

You own those ruby slippers now!

The ruby slippers from the story of *The Wizard of Oz* represent the philosopher's stone of alchemy. They serve to connect the limited to the unlimited. In the book, the slippers were silver to represent lead and the brick road was gold to represent the turning of lead into gold as an alchemist would.

In the movie version of the story that many of us love, we know the slippers to be Ruby in color, the reason for this was the invention of Technicolor, and red is a powerful color that gets our attention more than any other. How appropriate given that Dorothy's infinite powers are housed in the shoes, of course they should be in the powerful red, meant to get our attention fully and keep us enthralled for the entirety of the journey.

Dorothy knows that she is special because she's been awarded the shoes right when she lands in Munchkinland, but she doesn't know exactly how special she is or how infinite her powers are. She must go on a journey to remember who she truly is, the essence of her light being, her soul's purpose, her 'home'.

This is why Glinda couldn't share with her the magic of the ruby slippers when she first received them. Dorothy had to learn for herself exactly how powerful she was and so do you!

Ready to Click Your Heels?

Perhaps you have been ambivalent about slowing down, resistant to give in to your inner world, for fear of the results of leaving the safety of Kansas or Munchkinland.

Too often we find ourselves overly critical of our talents, our passions, our gifts or what interests us. And we stay safe in Kansas or Munchkinland, not even venturing out on our own yellow brick road or attempting to click our heels. And yet we have each been awarded a pair of ruby slippers and it is our Soul's purpose to click them and find our way home.

When you finally click your heels, you set yourself free to accept the power that is within you, the infinite power which elevates the energies of the Earth. Just as Dorothy was able to elevate the experience of the Munchkins by landing on the Wicked Witch of the East, so too do each of us elevate the energies of this Earth by clicking our heels finding our way home and then sharing that experience and wisdom with somebody else.

And just as with Dorothy, we feel overwhelmed by the responsibility of owning our ruby slippers and the power that they hold. We know in our hearts that we are meant to share something much bigger than who we currently are and yet, we allow the flying monkeys to hold us back, we fall asleep in the poppies, we fall prey to the false promises of the Wizards who say they can do it for us, and we lack the courage to take the action of pouring water on the Witch, as Dorothy did in order to prove herself worthy of clicking her heels and returning home.

In 3D, unlike in Oz, you may not feel the presence of your dear friends the Scarecrow, the Tin man, the Lion, and Toto; always at the ready to support you, celebrate you, and lock arms with you all the way through to the Emerald City and beyond. I often say to my clients **Cellar Seekers Beware**: The Journey to Oz is not for the faint of heart. Traveling your yellow brick road and clicking your heels to own your power, fully; your voice, your light, your gift to the world, is only for those brave enough to embrace the tornado, see themselves in others, pull the curtain back on the Wizards of life (even the internal ones), ask for help when they find themselves asleep in the poppies, and face the fear to pour water on the Witch and set themselves free.

The journey most often fought in our heads, our dreams, our illusions, can feel like a constant dark forest, fraught with danger, a never-ending spiral of challenges. Yet that same journey is the one that brings you straight to the ability to click your heels and release your infinite power.

Every trip to Oz is the next revolution of your evolution. Dorothy faces her fears, shares her voice, protects her friends (*the elements of her consciousness and pillars of manifestation*) and that is when Glinda the Good Witch - Dorothy's spirit guide and mentor - reveals to her that she has had the power to know herself (*return home*) ALL along. All she need do is remember her truth. And with all her fears released she is FREE to unlock her true power and find her way home.

Dorothy IS infinite LIGHT - the Paradigm shift!! An infinite unlimited being - all other elements are simply tools for her – the mind (Scarecrow), the heart (Tin Man), the courage to act (Lion), the intuition (Toto), the ego (Wicked Witch), the higher self (Glinda), and the soul's purpose (the ruby slippers). All come together on the yellow brick road to light the way for her to remember her authentic truth through the obstacles of society (Munchkins), role models (Kansas, Auntie Em and Uncle Henry), leaders (Wizard), and her own doubts (Flying Monkeys).

Let me now ask you... Do you feel as if you have been eternally waiting to integrate all aspects of your personality with your heart and your spirit to finally come to realize a sense of your inner purpose?

The fact that you are reading this book shows that you are in an active state of healing energy, starting to remember and accept the powerful light energy that you are which fuels your ruby slippers. It means that now is the time to discover the power of your ruby slippers and Click Your Heels!

The Gold at the End of the Rainbow – Abundance

Dorothy goes '*somewhere over the rainbow*' in search of what she thinks is a better life. Just as we often think that the 'grass is greener on the other side' and that surely with a location shift, we will be 'home'.

The thing of it is...the 'gold' at the end of the rainbow is not always as we originally thought. Many times the mass consciousness dictates the 'norm', the standards... wealth as represented by money, intelligence as represented by education, courage as represented by victory in an 'act of war', and love as represented by a heart, a token of appreciation. Remember how Dorothy thought that the Wizard was her answer that he would help to take her home? However, in the end all he could do was to give her and her friends a representation of their desires by societies standards (a medal, a diploma, a heart clock).

When each of us is willing to become aware, to wake up from the illusion, the dream state, we can recognize how we have created this wonderful role play and choose instead freedom through the embracing of our unique gifts as infinite beings of light. We find the 'gold at the end of the rainbow' is US. We are the light at the end of the tunnel that we have been seeking all along.

click your heels

Somewhere over the rainbow is not a place, it's a state of being, therein lies the true gold.

Put on those ruby slippers, go explore Oz, walk your yellow brick road. The adventure and your courage to act in every scene of Oz is the key for you to click your heels, manifest your dreams, and find your gold.

there's no place like home

Moral of the Story

There is no place like home... there is NO greater or more powerful gift than your TRUE SELF. We leave the heroic journey a changed person with a message for the world. What will be the moral of your story? What will you take form this revolution of your evolution?

The Moral of your Story...

In the Wonderful Wizard of Oz, the moral of the story is "*there is no place like home*" there is NO greater or more powerful gift than your TRUE SELF - your voice - and it's found within your heroic journey; your adventure to self-illumination.

A friend asked me as I was writing this, "*What was so great about the ending of the Wizard of Oz? After all,* she goes back to Kansas and nothing has changed, it's still drab, it's still mundane and the people are all in the same place with the same beliefs."

Ahhh, Jay, the beauty of this story is that DOROTHY has changed! She has found herself, she is 'home'. And we must all remember that our 'home' goes with us, no matter the physical location of our human being. The true gift in the heroic journey is finding Self and knowing that no matter where you find yourself, you will always be 'home'.

Dorothy had changed; therefore, everything around her was completely different from her new elevated perspective. The true gift of the story is to know as Confucius says, *"no matter where you go, there you are"* and if you are indeed connected to your own light, you are the gold over your own rainbow and can always be at 'home'.

"If I ever go looking for my heart's desire again, I won't look any further than my own back yard. Because if it isn't there, I never really lost it to begin with." – L. Frank Baum, The Wonderful Wizard of Oz

Do you know what 'home' is for you?

If home is your purpose, isn't your purpose then the mission and moral of 'your story' - your legacy - your voice?

And do you not feel most fulfilled and happy when you are home?

Remember the grey landscape and experience of Kansas is not about the physical structure or location... it is about BEING authentic, about being with those who most inspire your light and are inspired by your light. If you find yourself in Kansas right now, you are probably not living fully in your 'home', your authentic self, the heart of your power. Your existence may even feel a bit drab, monotone, and static.

If so, there you have the awareness and the tension to allow the tornado. If you were fulfilled completely, you'd have no desire to be, do, have, experience anything other than the present, the now. *Yet you want to be somewhere over the rainbow, don't you?*

Start Here

Don't know the moral of your story yet; your passion, your purpose in life? There's good news there is a solution to your problem and it's called your Heroic Journey. Your purpose is to be fulfilled and happy, to be 'home'. Cool right?

I always tell my clients to begin with the end in mind. You know where you are NOW... but where do you desire to BE and how will you feel when you get there?

What will 'home' feel like to you? What types of experiences might you have when you get there? How will you know you are there?

You have a trip to Oz up ahead, a yellow brick road yet to be revealed to you, and a host of friends awaiting the journey with you.

You have already established that your expectations no longer meet your expectancy, that you are in Kansas but not *of* it any longer, there's a storm a brewin' will you embrace the tornado this time?

Yes, some uncomfortable debris may be shed and there are bound to be periods of uncertainty and challenges but the gifts that await you when you put on those shoes is bound to be more than worth the wild ride!

next stop... home!

Now you have the Ruby Slipper Principles and can harness the infinite power of your divine spark and click your heels right home.

after oz

And then...

The consciousness of Kansas is elevated.

After her journey, Dorothy returns to Kansas, but what of that dull, dreary past 'home' of hers? Dorothy is changed but has anything else changed? Will Almira Gultch now embrace Toto? Will Auntie Em and Uncle Henry now rise up and take their authentic place as equal authorities and beings in the world? Will Huck, Hick and Zeke now see their own gifts and feel more secure? Will Professor Marvel learn to authentically use his intuition rather than trick others into paying him for his "wizardry"?

What does it mean for Dorothy to share her new found light and life? Is she now to preach on high and push her story on to others? Do everything she can to make the others 'see the light' of the error of their ways? OR will living in her authenticity, holding space for others to walk their own yellow brick road, and continually shining the light for them, be the best way to unleash her ruby slippers.

Too often when we have a life-altering and eye-opening experience like Oz we are excited to share it with others and to have them join us in our new 'awakening'. Its true of those who convert to a new religion, or away from a former religion, or who find divination or reveal new information about the government that has them both reeling back and propelled forward with new vigor. But, what course of action is best for Kansas? What is best for the collective consciousness?

My purpose for writing this book was certainly to help you find your soul's purpose, overcome your doubts and unleash your inner power. However, it was also to elevate the energies of the Earth by raising awareness and the collective consciousness.

So how does clicking your own heels help the whole of the Earth?

Let me go back just a bit to help us go forward. In 2012, many of us thought the apocalypse was upon us, "*the end of the world as we know it*", certainly at a minimum a big tipping point for the energies here on Earth. And for many it has felt like a tornado ride ever since that point. Certainly, most of us have felt the disorienting swirl of being turned upside down by the 2016 election of Donald Trump in the United States. More and more that has called to the surface many lightworkers, healers, leaders of a new consciousness and expression to Click their Heels in a big way. I know you've felt it, it's why you are here right now.

However, that shift has not made everybody ready to ascend at the same time has it? We've found Cellar Seekers and lots of folks who are stuck in Munchkinland and equally we've found some very dark forests with nasty Flying Monkeys and Wicked (very wicked) Witches who seek to steal our freedom, our imagination and our minds. It's as real as it gets, or at least as real as I've experienced on my time here on Earth.

We are feeling most intimately the warning I share on my site and with my clients, the alert that Oz is NOT for everyone at this time. Don't get me wrong; it is certainly available to all of us and we are welcome to ride the tornado and grab our shoes but, it's just NOT easy to release the cellar doors, face the witch and go through the adventure of spiritual alchemy. Those are shoes that come with profound responsibilities and powers.

As you realize your true value, your worth, your power, you will be ascending and awakening. Others around you may not be quite ready to go there with you. Your true gift to humanity rests with your ability to allow them to BE exactly where they are on their journey and to do so without judgment or force and with the utmost love, compassion and forgiveness for the part that they are taking in this vast evolution.

In 2012, I read a passage in a book called *"2012: The Mayan Sunrise"* that has stayed with me for years and inspired my trajectory in life. *To paraphrase, it was noted that for each lightworker* (person willing to click his/her heels and unleash their own power and light) *who was willing to shine their light into the world; they would create space for 100,000 other souls to evolve and join us in the ascension.* THAT is powerful stuff! That means, that just by clicking your heels in an intentional space of allowing, understanding and compassion... YOU will create the space for the ascension of 100,000 other souls to ascend to Oz IN THEIR OWN TIME and WAY! If that's not a reason to click your heels then I certainly don't know what is.

How to Elevate the Energies of the Earth with Your Ruby Slippers

But, how can you do that in the way that creates that powerful space for ascension; to create the opening for your 100,000 souls to join us? The secret to that lies in detachment from it.

Remember that the adventure off to Oz starts when your expectations no longer meet your expectancy. Expectations can really start a swirly emotional tornado. And when we are talking about other people and desperately wanting them to join us on our ascension and awakening, very few will ever be able to meet your expectations. Rather than become frustrated with them or to pull them from their cellar doors, it will serve you best to go back to a state of expectancy RATHER than expectation.

Expectancy – the state of thinking that something pleasant will occur or come to be. An anticipatory desire if you will.

Expectation – a belief that someone '*should*' be, do or desire something.

Let's take this back to Oz... Dorothy upon her return to Kansas would likely LOVE to experience the awakening and ascension of Auntie Em and Uncle Henry (certainly she'd LOVE for Almira Gultch to 'see the light' as it relates to Toto). Where she will be unsuccessful is in her expectation that they have or will ascend simply because she has. It will serve her much better (and the Earth for that matter) if she simply returns to Kansas with expectancy – the expectancy that Auntie Em and Uncle Henry will still LOVE her and be overjoyed that she has come back unharmed from being swept up in a tornado.

And what of her relationship to the archetypes in Oz? Will she be best served to hold on to anger and resentment toward Almira Gultch for trying to take Toto from her, for trying to steal her ruby slippers while in Oz? Perhaps face Almira now in her elevated state of being and debate with her to see things from a new perspective, maybe get her to open up a dog rescue.

Is she best to be upset that the Munchkins never left Munchkinland and didn't have the courage to walk the yellow brick road with her? To expect that they 'should' have seen the light and risen up to kill the Witch all on their own.

How will it turn out if she goes back to Professor Marvel and tells him she knows he's a fraud and he MUST live authentically from here on out because if he does, he will get a pair of ruby slippers and regain the love and admiration of all of Oz!

Despite her enthusiasm and new found 'truth'; her expectations for ANY of these archetypes will NOT be enough to create the space for them to ascend to Oz. Instead, in her enthusiasm, she creates resistance and sends them all right back to the cellar doors, alienating them from her instead of endearing them to her. Think about it – she's just the crazy girl who got a bump on her head and created a conspiracy theory while she was 'out of it.' Poor dear.

Now let's bring this back to real life. Here in reality, post the 2012 apocalypse and 2016 Presidential election, the great tipping point on Earth (and I do believe it is a significant tipping point but, that's a story for another time). How can you help others to awaken and arise with you so that they too can live a life-fulfilled?

1. *Release* expectation and embrace expectancy. Living from an energy of faith and love rather than obligation or fear.

2. *Forgive* yourself and others. For any actions taken, words spoken, beliefs embraced while under the spell of the hypnotic rhythm.

3. *Allow* yourself and others to continually evolve. That includes accepting new perspectives, changing your mind as new things are revealed, and doing so in a space of non-judgement and unconditional love.

By clicking your heels in this way, you ARE creating the space for 100,000 others to join you; in their own time, in their own way! The Scarecrow, Tinman and Lion didn't each get their own pair of ruby slippers but they certainly experienced spiritual alchemy and their own unique revelations, awakenings and ascension.

And remember, the Witch is dissolved in Oz, but she is still present here in Kansas when Dorothy returns. However, with Dorothy's new-found powers, her perception of self and home; she will react to Almira Gultch in a completely different way - their energies now will likely not clash like they once did. In fact, I think Dorothy will be more apathetic towards Almira, and vice versa. Because the energies have completely shifted, and the energetic discords have been severed.

We will know that we've come to a place of expectancy when we are no longer 'triggered' by the people and situations we once were. We will have found a new 'home'.

A New Yellow Brick Road for Kansas

Don't get me wrong; even in Kansas you'll be challenged. *The Wizards* will still try to sell you illusions - always remind yourself to peek behind their curtains before you accept the initial offering; be discerning of the narratives you are hearing from 'leaders'.

And the Witches will still try to program you with clever marketing to take control of your free thinking, therefore be discerning about what you are being told to fear, accept, and enjoy.

And the Munchkins will most certainly entice you to stay with them, therefore be discerning of social norms and pressures which may show up through likes and retweets and lots of social love.

If you will pause to simply observe the world, watch from a detached state of being, as a neutral witness with infinite curiosity – you will see how the archetypes show up in your everyday life.

Please keep in mind that all the archetypes of Oz are within us and are us. We are truly One. So, to allow the forgiveness, love and acceptance of every part of your Self (and therefore others) is truly how we will all be able to awaken from the dream (4D) and ascend to a much more conscious state of being. Rather than express your fear through anger, your resentment through resistance or your discontent through debate – why not rise above to a place of expectancy and then draw others in to that space of love?

It is my hope that you will return from this adventure armed with new perspectives and a shiny pair of ruby slippers. And with those you will truly see things much differently and react to them from a place of intentional and detached witness and curiosity. Rather than engaging Almira Gultch in a debate about why it is important for her to spend her money on a dog rescue, simply allow her to be in her own space and journey; perhaps she will grow to love Toto and perhaps she NEVER will – either outcome will now be neutral to you because you have clicked your heels and have no expectations for her to be anything other than who she is and where she is. Perhaps she's had a long and fearful life in the hypnotic rhythm and does not yet feel ready to sing her own song; let's hold space for her and respect that.

I assure you that by taking responsibility for owning and unleashing the power of your ruby slippers – you will SEE your experience changed.

You will notice Kansas becoming more colorful, joyful and awakened.

You will no longer feel the need to 'battle the Witch' for you will have already overcome that challenge within yourself.

Your new 'home' will feel more peaceful and freeing with every passing day.

And even though you will still find the Almiras of the World out to get your dog – your reaction to them will be much different – you will not feel as agitated; nor the desire to fight or convert them – instead you will remember to diffuse them with a bit of love and compassion and let them go on their way.

***

thank you

I can't thank you enough for sharing this sacred space with me and allowing me to express an old favorite story in a new inspirulluminated way. It is my hope that these principles and the Oznalogy have inspired you to explore your yellow brick road and click your heels.

'til we meet again in Oz,

~Glinda

p.s. As an independent publisher, word of mouth and referrals are priceless to me. If you have enjoyed this adventure, I would be very grateful to you if you would share it with others who you think might enjoy the experience. How? I'd love for you to review it on Amazon, loan or gift the book to a friend, or share your insights and thoughts on social media using #rubyslipperprinciples. I welcome your thoughts and invitations to discuss.

an interview with glinda

An interview with Loreen Muzik (Glinda) by Tabitha Dial

Tabitha: *What came first: The call to do intuitive readings/coaching for others, or the desire to work with the world of the Wizard of Oz?*

Glinda: *Oz came first.* I'm a story teller at heart; an imaginative soul, a creative being; reading and writing were my escape when I was young. I tend to speak in analogies and allegories and the world opens up to me as I do.

About 6 years ago I was working with the concept of the heroic journey and I was searching my intuitive archives for an analogy to share with a client. Instantly, *The Wonderful Wizard of Oz* came to me. That evening the

Oznalogy and the language of Oz which would become the foundation for my soul's work, was created.

Tarot followed shortly after my fascination with exploring Oz in a new way. After sharing the Oznalogy with my client so that she could have a better understanding of her own heroic journey, she sent me a lovely gift... a deck of tarot cards. She said I'd be wonderful at reading them and felt called to gift them to me.

I have always been intuitive, claircognizant primarily, so accessing my imagination as the gateway to intuition felt natural to me. Tarot reading then became a natural extension to my coaching practice and the concept of Oz for me.

My guidance philosophy revolves around using various forms of divination for self-exploration, self-development and strategies to help you improve your life and live more fulfilled. I purposefully focus on empowering you to take advantage of the pathways and options that are best for you; much like the advice that Glinda provided to Dorothy along her journey.

Just as Dorothy had Toto to guide her, we have divination. From Toto to tarot to transformation, the connection for me between the two worlds has been both seamless and reinforcing. I've been guiding my clients and reading tarot since the receipt of that wonderful gift and my love of helping Dorothy's navigate the yellow brick roads of life through tarot was born.

I have expanded my practice to include Akashic Records readings and conducting guided yellow brick road tours (both group and individual). Finding that awareness of our fears and obstacles is one great step in the right direction, getting Glinda to sprinkle a little snow on us to release some energy blocks helps us to get back up and move more swiftly toward clicking our heels. The guidance I can receive from the Akashic Records and the energy healing work done as a result of that are just the snow my Dorothy's have been needing to help wake them up from the poppies.

Tabitha: *I love the straightforwardness of your disclaimer on your site:*

"FAIR WARNING: Cellar Seekers may want to stay in Kansas – Oz is ONLY for the brave of heart and those willing to engage in self-involvement and self-evolvement. You don't ever have to travel your yellow brick road alone but, you will have to be willing to step out of the house once that tornado lands you in Oz!"

Please expand on this statement, particularly how you define self-involvement and self-evolvement.

Glinda: *Self-involvement and self-evolvement to me are a willingness to engage with and be a witness to oneself.* To become intimately and actively engaged with your own spiritual development, and to use the knowledge and wisdom gained from that experience to evolve, to expand your perceptions, to elevate your resonance and to heighten your spiritual consciousness.

The tornado that swoops Dorothy up and off to Oz is the bridge from consciousness to higher consciousness and in the shape of a spiral – the divine sequence of nature, the Fibonacci sequence. It is the shape of our DNA, the shape of the trajectory of our very planet through space. It represents the revolution of the evolution of our being, our consciousness.

I say Cellar Seekers may want to stay in Kansas because...let's face it, not everyone is ready for the 'Oz' journey... to face the monkeys... to desire to know oneself so deeply that we are willing to go into battle with the Witch/Ego. Sometimes it's just much easier for us to stay asleep in the poppies or live among the fantasies of lollipops and gumdrops in Munchkinland where all appears blissfully happy on the outside and we'd much rather have others fight our battles for us.

What's that they say... when the hero is ready the challenge and courage will appear. Well, ok no they don't say that but, you can see why understanding that this adventure is self-involved, a deeply intimate and insightful work and it's not for everybody at this time. Each of us is ready in our own time. If the disclaimer seems off-putting to a potential client then, they will know that this is not the time for their work with me. I'm ok with that. I'd rather let you know that there are challenges up ahead than to feed you lollipops and gumdrops like the Munchkins.

That's not to say that the adventure can't be fun and filled with laughter and support and encouragement and GROWTH because it will be.

Tabitha: *What makes your guidance a gift for the brave of heart?*

Glinda: *Each of us can relate to the idea of wanting to know who we truly are...* what our purpose is in life... what our unique powers and voice can hold... and we can relate to being afraid to face our fears in order to achieve our ultimate dreams. We want to click our heels and return home! But too often we cannot see what we cannot witness, we do not know what we do not know or remember, and the journey feels more dizzying than evolutionary.

Divination acts as a phenomenal witness to our very being. A guidance session can highlight the flying monkeys on your journey, it can show you if you are headed to the

Emerald City or the Dark Forest, or if you have encountered a Wizard who seeks to deceive you. Likewise, it can illuminate your support system, your Scarecrow thoughts, your Tin man passions, and your courage to take inspired action like the Lion. Folks can find out what to leave behind in Kansas as well as some encouraging inspiration and advice from Glinda who is always there to sprinkle a little snow if you've fallen asleep in the poppies.

The gift is that once you are awake to the elements of your current trajectory, it becomes much easier to release your blocks, get out of your own way and begin taking steps toward living a life fulfilled.

At a minimum, you'll be able to defeat a few of those flying monkeys. You may even be able to finally pour water on the witch who seeks to take the power of your ruby slippers for herself. And as you continue to navigate your yellow brick road, you can reveal and understand the unique pattern to click your heels and find your way 'home'.

What I have shared with you here is a sneak peek behind my own curtain, a glimpse of the passion project that I have been working on for quite some time.

My love of Oz continues to expand and express itself through my being and business. Every day I am fascinated by the twists and turns of my yellow brick road and charmed by the delightful beings I meet who expand my experience and consciousness.

I have made it my mission to share with others how to go from Kansas to Clicking Your Heels and passion-it-forward to elevate the energies of the earth.

Tabitha: *What is a Yellow Brick Road Tour!?*

Glinda: *Yellow Brick Road Tours are a total immersion into the elements of your soul, with in-depth intuitive guidance and support so that you can: align with all the archetypes of Oz, illuminate your personal path to life-fulfilled and reveal the infinite power held in your ruby slippers.*

My divination and guidance for these sessions comes from both Tarot and Akashic Records readings, customized for you to help you defeat the flying monkeys of doubt, wake up from the addictive/distractions of sleepy time in the poppies and harness the courage to have full awareness of your shadows and then pour water on that Witch to release it and begin the healing process!

Through this adventure you will reveal and unleash the infinite power within you, your soul's purpose, with Glinda by your side. A joyful discovery of your inner being, a personalized path to your life-fulfilled and revelation of what keeps you in Kansas or

Munchkinland and how to OVERCOME that so you can click your heels.

I am also launching group tours in 2019. Together we will discover our yellow brick roads, empower and support one another to take courageous steps forward AND learn how to do a little self-navigation work through your connection to your higher self and your intuition.

We use tarot and oracles; but don't worry if you don't know tarot yet... it's fun and easy and anyone can do it... you'll love it as a navigation tool and I'll teach you what you need to know. If you think you'd like to be a part one of these tours please get on the invitation list now!

Tabitha: *Why work with you?*

Glinda: *Because, you know you are meant for so much more.* And yet... you are either bitter or frustrated by your lack of progress in creating your ideal life, vision or business. You may have even tried to put yourself out there yet somehow you just couldn't gain traction.

Why?

It's NOT because:

- You're not capable of making it happen – that's just a doubtful mind Scarecrow

- You're not passionate about creating a dream life — that's just a jaded heart Tin man
- You don't have enough time or money to pursue your dreams — that's just a cowardly excuse Lion

You have everything you need to manifest your life fulfilled!

It's because:

You don't have CLARITY on your yellow brick road! You need to know your WHO, WHAT and HOW!

- WHO you are meant to be
- WHAT you are meant to create and offer the world
- HOW you are going to do that

And despite trying diligently by reading books and blogs, buying course after course, and learning modality after modality... you just can't figure it out all on your own. Let's face it; Oz is quite an adventure to navigate! There are hidden obstacles everywhere from the limiting beliefs of Kansas, to the small thinking Munchkins, flying monkeys of doubt to the false promises of Wizards.

Good news! Dorothy had Glinda for the journey and so can you! I know that you are a heroine! A ruby slipper wearin', heel clickin' passion filled pioneer!

But... you've found yourself:

- stuck in Kansas, living in monotony

- *exhausted by the Executive Witch trying to steal your shoes*
- completely done with the Coaching Wizards making false promises
- *plagued by Flying monkeys trying to sabotage your dreams*
- successful in so many ways and yet feeling unfulfilled...
- *and you are looking for the right place to get your new shoes and a little direction toward the gold over your rainbow.*

Am I right? Because let me tell you I've been there and so wished that Glinda would have told me the secrets to clicking my heels!

I help heroes and heroines struggling with uncertainty, questioning their self-worth and searching for the courage to fulfill their life's purpose, to trust their inner voice, uncover their true value and take inspired and courageous action toward a life fulfilled; all through the magic of 'The Wonderful Wisdom of Oz'.

If you're ready for a yellow brick road tour then I'll share this secret with you... you'll be faced with flying monkeys, dark forests, at least one witch who seeks to take your power and wizards who will want to keep you in a land of illusion. It's going to be great to know that you've got a good witch on your side! Plus, it's just darn fun!

But don't just take my word for it, lots of other folks have enjoyed the adventure!

"*I've just had an extensive (yellow brick road tour) with you that was so necessary in my life right now that I cannot begin to tell you. You were straight to the point and pulled no punches, that's for sure! Loreen, you were so kind and understanding. You were not only able to peer deeply into my soul and circumstances, oh no. You also helped show the path before me as well as the way to clear it. The entire experience was so above and beyond in my book. I will certainly be referring to the recording of our reading again and again - there was just so much useful information! This session turned out to be one hell of a prescription, and I thank you deeply for your help. You are providing a truly good service to others.*" - Sarah P. Edmonton, Canada

"*I honestly am crying at how on-point you are with this! Please let this serve as affirmation that you have a beautiful talent. Loreen, I know that you will do great things, and by helping others to heal, you are fulfilling part of your life's purpose. Such a blessing you are, and how lucky we are to have you here in this lifetime...you are a bright and beautiful soul! From my heart to yours, thank you for this!*" - Much love and light, Kimberly

Tabitha: *How can folks work with you?*

Glinda: *There are 3 ways to work with me:* 1:1 mentoring and guidance, group and DIY courses. Whether you want a guided personal tour of your yellow brick road, someone to help you build your emerald city or you'd like to learn how to read tarot as your navigation tool... I can help.

I invite folks to visit my site at GlindasGuidance.com to inquire about my services.

In addition to coaching, I plan to release my second book "***From Toto to Tarot*** *– a Good Witches Guide to Unleashing Your Intuition*" as well as accompanying online course(s) learn how to navigate the yellow brick road for yourself and others.

***

My sincere gratitude to Tabitha Dial for this insightful interview and for permission to re-publish it here in *The Ruby Slipper Principles*. She also asked about how I best connect to Toto and that answer became Ruby Slipper Principle #2 – feed toto – thank you for that inspiration Tabitha!

Tabitha is a creative diviner who uses tarot, tea leaves and poetry to develop her personal code. She is a brilliant author and her latest book: *"Creative Divination: Read Tea Leaves and Develop Your Personal Code"* can be found on Amazon. For more information please visit her at: NorthStarMuse.com

***

about the author

Loreen Muzik a former HR Executive, has been using her intuitive coaching skills to guide others to the source of their inner power for more than 25 years. In 2009 an Executive Witch stole her ruby slippers, kicked her out of corporate Oz and sent her reeling back to Kansas confused about whether or not she had a brain, heart or the courage to move on. Seeking a new yellow brick road, Loreen pursued a certification in life coaching, Tarot reading and the Akashic Records. Today, she incorporates her 3D, 4D and 5D modalities to help others see the power of their ruby slippers through the wonderful wisdom of Oz.

Originally from the Chicagoland area of Illinois, Loreen now splits her time between the charming Traverse City, Michigan and Highland Park, Illinois with her husband, Jerry and her adorable Corgis vanGogh and

Matisse and Ragdoll kitty, Kipu. When she's not writing books or creating new courses/workshops, she can be found reading great books on the couch, collecting tarot cards and further exploring the world of divination.

Contact Loreen

Visit: www.GlindasGuidance.com
Email: loreen@glindasguidance.com

work with loreen

Want to work with me?

Visit: GlindasGuidance.com

Want to take a Yellow Brick Road Tour?

Get on the invitation list for the next tour.

Visit: WonderfulWisdomofOz.com

Made in the USA
Middletown, DE
24 March 2019